Grief Is Dark, But It Can Lighten

When the Death of a Loved One Appears Impassable

Jesse Montanya

Table of Contents

Introduction

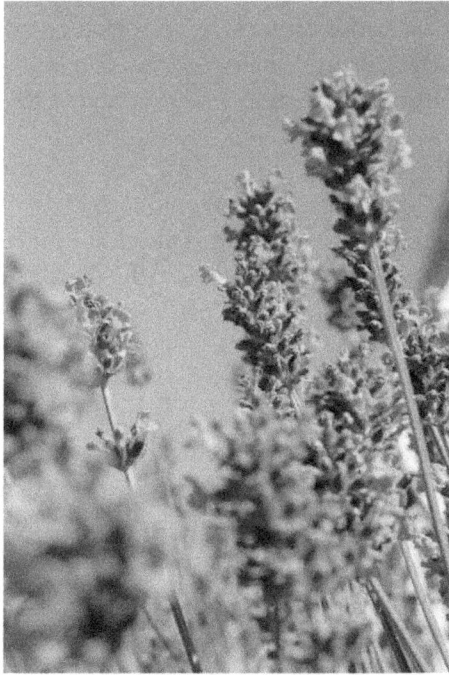

Lavender: Calming properties, symbolizes peace, tranquility, purity, serenity

I have been a professional counselor in Australia for over 20 years. My skills were honed by the demographic of my clients. The first decade of my career was mostly spent helping individuals, families, and communities cope through the most devastating drought this country has ever experienced.

It was the first decade of the new millennium—a dark period for the primary producers of this country. The crops were decimated, livestock wiped out, communities shattered, and this was happening year after year. The toll that the drought took was devastating for the people, but the anguish and heartache of facing the uncertain future continued after the drought broke. It was tough to be one of the people who had to face this turmoil and help the people suffering from it.

I conducted my work in the most remote outback regions of Australia. It wasn't typical counseling in which an individual would come to me with an issue for guidance. Often, doctors would ask me to go out and see someone in need. I received many phone calls most weeks. Most were from women who were distraught and desperate for someone to help their husbands and partners. I conducted my appointments in shearing sheds, out repairing fencing, in my truck at watering points, or checking on livestock. I would go wherever my client felt most comfortable.

The world typically pictures Australians as tough, hardened, resilient, and resourceful individuals. Often this identity is associated with farmers and other people who care for the land. "Toughen the fuck up" was a common saying these people used to get themselves through difficult times.

I had to develop a counseling style that was able to break through their attitude of simply not asking for help. Traditionally, Australians have had a certain isolation from other countries, and historically this has created a certain independence of thought and behavior. It was difficult to work within generational, ingrained belief systems that would never permit seeking counseling. It was just not in their character. But then, nature forced their hand.

My work has been multifaceted, involving one-on-one or group counseling, community development, courses and seminars, workshops, and guest speaking to promote mental health and prevent mental illness.

For 20 years, I have described my work like this: Professional counseling is a privilege when someone so desperately in need invites you into their life. They need you to address serious issues simply because they cannot. There is no greater privilege!

Now, I want to share my experiences and knowledge to help a greater population to heal.

Grief is a journey that can only be truly understood by those who tread its path. I stand beside you, a fellow traveler through that journey.

In acknowledging your pain, I freely offer my empathy. Together, we'll find a way through the corridors of grief. When despair hangs heavy and the weight of the world threatens to engulf you, I'll be with you. Even in the darkest moments, I will remain by your side.

My intention is not to be clinical or detached but to extend a hand to you in your sorrow. I won't mince words; this is a challenging topic infused with a sense of the rawness that mirrors your own. I've crafted my words to foster not just understanding but genuine transformation. Let me assure you that, although the road ahead is difficult, you need not journey alone. Walking this path with you is an honor and a privilege.

Your feelings are unique, a tapestry woven from experiences, memories, and emotions that are yours alone. Your grief, too, is individual, a range of emotions that change you in ways only you can know. The death of someone you hold dear can shatter your spirit, leaving you adrift. But because of our shared experience of loss, I can be a guide through pain.

During this voyage, there will be challenges. The experience of grief can be relentless but remember that I am here. Every page you read is a recognition of your courage and a step toward healing.

This book isn't an exhaustive manual of grief's most intricate facets. I won't prescribe strategies to instantly ease your pain. Grief isn't an illness to be cured; it's a process that requires time and self-awareness. My aim is to empower you with understanding and to encourage you to express what you need to—when you're ready.

The more complex instances of grief resulting from traumatic deaths like murder and suicide will find their space in another volume in this series. For now, the focus rests on the grief that follows the loss of a loved one.

In this book, I hope to share my experiences and insights in order to facilitate healing and growth for readers dealing with their own experiences of grief. This is a mutual journey, a shared exploration of grief's terrain. And as we move forward together, know that you're not alone. Grief is a formidable adversary, but I believe in the potential for transformation.

Thank you for allowing me to join you on your journey.

Note: I have included one of the international flowers of peace with each chapter. Pause and read the caption. See the beauty. Feel the peace.

Part 1:

The Shock

Chapter 1:

The Consuming State of Shock

White poppy: Remembrance events and celebration of life, renewal, peace and calmness

The grief that you feel over the death of a loved one is completely understandable. It's normal and natural. Grief is a complex emotional response to the death of a loved one—someone who has been significant in your life. The fact that grief is so complicated can leave you with any number of distressing feelings. They can even be devastating.

Shock, denial, and disbelief are common reactions to the trauma of a death in the first days after it occurs. There is no specific pattern in which these responses will appear. A person may experience denial or disbelief before shock sets in. Disbelief may come first. Shock is all too likely to be the first thing that you feel, though. All three reactions are natural, no matter in what order you experience them. Other emotions that you may feel include sadness, anger, confusion, and anxiety.

Grief comes to everyone in a different shape and time. It's important to remember that. Whatever the pattern is for you is how your mind reacts to the tragic event. Whatever you feel, whether it's anger, disbelief, being overwhelmed, sadness, or a combination of emotions you can't describe, your own feelings are valid. How you deal with them is unique to you as well.

The State of Shock

Although you may not realize what is happening to you when you experience the trauma of a death, one common reaction is shock. You may experience this as a sense of disbelief or denial. The sorrow of losing one close to you is simply too enormous a feeling to be believed. Even if you knew the person's death was coming, as with a parent who is old and very ill, shock still exists.

You may view the person's body, now empty of the life and personality you once treasured about them. Or perhaps you are merely informed of the death. However you first learn of the death, you always wish for one more moment of life, the opportunity to tell your loved one just one more thing. You may experience the event happening in a fog, as a sense of unreality.

What you are feeling is shock that is compounded by disbelief and denial. I'll guide you through these reactions in this chapter. Just know that the feelings are a natural response to death. Just because you feel this way, you are not taking the death too hard or overdramatizing.

Shock is both an emotion and a natural physical reaction. Both your body and brain experience the event and have different ways of processing it. Your brain experiences sensations of overwhelming emotions, including profound distress. Your body may react by crying, trembling, or feeling sick. Both of these experiences are part of the phenomenon called shock.

Twelve years ago, I was in a catastrophic truck accident. My upper body was crushed. I was critically injured and in the ICU for six days. One of my most vivid memories is how, just as the truck pulled me under the engine block, there was an automatic shut-off in my mind. My vision went, but I could still hear. I was conscious at first, but just when most of the damage was being done to my body, my mind switched off and I felt no pain. It was a split second, but it's a vivid memory to this day. I pulled through, and after several surgeries and years of treatment, I have all normal function back.

Twenty-five years earlier, I had experienced the same effects after the sudden and tragic death of my wife. I wasn't aware of life around me. Sometimes the entire morning would pass, and I had no idea of what I had done. I recall these experiences as a quite terrifying void—just a blank. That was the brain's intention—to keep this "vessel" alive.

As one of the symptoms of grief, from either a sudden or expected death of someone young or old, the processing and reasoning part of the brain can shut down. This is due to psychological shock.

The Two Kinds of Shock

I researched an explanation for what I'd experienced during my accident and was amazed. The front part of the brain—the prefrontal cortex—is the consciousness, the processing and reasoning section of the brain. When a traumatic experience happens, a person enters a fight, flight, or freeze state, which can result in the prefrontal cortex shutting down.

There are two different kinds of shock that a person can experience: physiological shock and psychological shock. Physiological shock is a condition that affects the body. When the accident first did damage to my body, I went into physiological shock. The symptoms occur when there is not enough blood traveling to the organs, so they begin to shut down.

If this shock doesn't lead to death, there are other symptoms that can arise. Your pulse can be rapid or weak; your breathing may be rapid or shallow; you may have dilated pupils; you could have cool, clammy skin; or you could have confusion or lose consciousness. This was what I first experienced.

Psychological shock, on the other hand, happens when you undergo a severe, emotionally traumatic event that usually occurs unexpectedly. Your body releases adrenaline, a hormone that has specific effects, too. You can feel like you're going to vomit. Your thinking may be affected, so you can't think straight. You could feel intense anger. Or, like I did, you can dissociate—feel detached from your body, like you're not really there but numb all over.

When human beings were at an early stage of development, that surge of adrenaline could save their lives if they were threatened by a wild animal. They would have one of three reactions. They could flee, running away from the danger. They could try to fight the predator. Or they could freeze, becoming immobile, perhaps in hope that the threat wouldn't see them move or because they were simply unable to move their limbs.

Unfortunately, those reactions don't work so well in modern life, where physical threats aren't so common. Adrenaline affects us anyway. We still flee, fight, or freeze in reaction to it. The adrenaline that surges through your body can make you run away from your feelings, become angry, or shut down. You can experience life as eerily slowed down or frighteningly sped up.

Shock is dangerous to the brain and body. You may feel actual, physical pain as your body goes into psychological shock because of the stress hormones flooding your system. As with physiological shock, you may feel tightness in your throat or chest, a rapid or slowed heartbeat, or shortness of breath. While the shock lasts, the pain may be deferred, but it will come eventually.

Prolonged shock can actually be physically harmful. It sets up a stress reaction like the one you experience when you're in a situation you can't escape from, such as prolonged physical abuse that can lead to post-traumatic stress disorder. You feel overwhelmed, with a need to take control despite an inability to do so. You can feel lonely and depressed or bad about yourself in general.

Physical symptoms can occur, too. You can develop migraine headaches, insomnia, sexual dysfunction, or changes in appetite. Prolonged stress can affect your brain functions, bringing on racing thoughts, disorganization, and pessimism. Your behavior may change, with you increasing use of drugs or alcohol, eating too much or too little, or avoiding responsibilities.

Eventually, though, you will move into other phases in your reaction to grief.

Disbelief

"She can't be dead. She was so young!"

"But he was feeling better just last week!"

"I thought the doctors would save him!"

These are all ways of saying, "I don't believe my loved one is really dead."

The reality of death is hard to accept when it happens to someone you know and love.

Along with disbelief go guilt and anger. There's a tendency to feel that you are somehow responsible for the death, even if in reality there was nothing you could do. *They wouldn't have been crossing that intersection at the wrong time if I had just talked to them a little longer*, you may think. *I shouldn't have left his bedside to get something to eat.* None of these actions would really have prevented the death, but you tell yourself they would have.

Disbelief is a way to temporarily get through the awful feelings that accompany death. It protects you from pain, at least for a while. The feelings seep through anyway. You find yourself crying at unexpected moments, even seemingly ordinary ones that have nothing to do with the death. You may become irritable and snap at the people around you. Small talk and everyday tasks can seem unendurable. *Ella should be here*, you think. *She would have really appreciated that joke.*

When you're in the disbelief stage of grief, it's impossible to imagine that everything will someday be okay again. All you can see is the void that has appeared in your life. You can't face seeing it, so you simply refuse to believe it is there. Sometimes disbelief is so strong that you find yourself feeling paradoxical emotions. People have been known to break into hysterical laughter—not because the death is funny but simply because their feelings are so unacceptable to them.

Denial

Denial is another common reaction to the death of a loved one, especially if the death is a sudden one. It's a form of dissociation. If you don't believe it's true, then it won't be. Of course, that doesn't work, but denial puts your emotions on hold for a while. You simply push them aside so that you don't have to feel them yet. It makes you feel better for a time. You can negotiate the many tasks you must do without feeling the emotions associated with them. You don't really believe that your loved one isn't dead. You simply deny that the death has a negative effect on you.

You say to yourself, "I can make the necessary phone calls. I can get through making the arrangements for the funeral. I can write the obituary for the paper. I can choose the music. I won't break down."

You make yourself function as if you were a robot with no feelings at all. Denial is a defense mechanism, protecting you from feelings that you fear are too big for you and too dangerous to let loose. Feeling nothing feels safer than releasing all the pain inside you. Deep down, you're afraid of what you might do—cry, scream, throw things, lash out in anger, hurt others. Of course, pushing your feelings aside doesn't make either them or the reality of death go away. They're still present, just waiting to resurface. And when they do, you may be in trouble.

When your grieving process goes on for a long time, it's known as "complicated grief." This condition results when the grief goes unresolved for an extended period of time. Of course, the amount of time required to recover from grief is individual to the person, but if someone shows no signs of recovery, they may be suffering from complicated grief.

This is an ongoing, heightened state of grieving that prevents you from moving ahead to where your feelings can be resolved. In some people, this may take months. In others, it may take a year or more. It does no good to expect someone to get over a death in what you consider to be an appropriate amount of time.

Complicated grief can be recognized when a bereaved person dwells on the life and death of the loved one. They may obsess about reminders of the person's life or ignore them altogether. Although, ordinarily, someone who's experienced the death of a loved one treasures memories of the good times they've shared, someone in complicated grief may not be able to remember them. Bitterness or a lack of trust in others may occur. In extreme cases, they may believe that life has no meaning.

Feel to Heal

Shock, denial, and disbelief are all ways that the brain tries to avoid feeling after tragic events. Unfortunately, healing can only occur after the affected person feels those feelings and processes them. While they're still avoiding their feelings, their emotions can't be resolved, and they can't reach a place of understanding.

This healing takes time, though how much time it will take is unpredictable. If a loved one has gone through a tragic bereavement, you can't force them to address their feelings. All you can do is hold space for them until they heal on their own. The way you do this is to be present for them and not try to hurry the process. You don't—can't—know the depth of the person's grief or truly understand their feelings, even if you have lost a loved one yourself.

You may see the person demonstrate the symptoms of shock, denial, or disbelief, but different people will experience them in a different way, in a different order, or for a different amount of time. It's best not to interfere or try to speed up the process. If you try to rush the person, you may actually be hindering how and when they arrive at healing.

The raw emotions a bereaved person is experiencing can make them lose awareness of the world around them. They may not feel hunger or thirst. They could neglect their own self-care, forgetting that they need to sleep—or they may sleep too much as an escape from their pain. As they experience the overwhelming feelings that go with loss, they may be terrified at the extent of their suffering. Their physical health and well-being, as well as their mental health, can deteriorate.

Although the person's pain may be alarming to their friends and family members, there is little they can do. Don't even try to fix the person. You can't. At this point, all a loved one can do is to keep the bereaved person safe. Someone in the depths of pain and despair can harm themself, usually unintentionally. They may stop eating, for example. You can try to help them by preparing meals for them, but don't be surprised if they push it away. Do try to make sure they eat at least a little something and drink water or juice to keep hydrated. Don't make a big deal of it. Don't try to coax them ("Come on, you've got to eat!") Instead, provide simple, healthful food and drinks, and let them take as much as they want to, even if that's only a few bites.

Another part of keeping the person safe is allowing them a space in which they can express their feelings. Don't shame or blame them, even if you don't understand why they feel the way they do. Don't try to talk them out of it. That will only slow down their healing. Trying to cheer them up is not going to work. Even talking about good memories you have of the person who died may not be helpful. It may remind the person that those good times are gone, never to return. And trying to coax them out of their sorrow is more likely to do harm than good.

Your presence can aid in healing, at least soon after the shock sets in. But the person may also prefer to be alone. If this goes on for more than a few days, though, they may be in a state of denial, ignoring or suppressing their feelings. It can help if you check in on them from time to time, allowing them the opportunity to express those feelings if they're ready to.

When you do visit someone who has suffered a loss, though, don't say things that you may think are encouraging. "You'll be all right." "You'll get through this." "Everything will be okay." The person won't believe these statements yet. Your attempted words of comfort won't get through because they won't line up with how the person is feeling. It's better to say, "I'm here for you." "It's safe for you to let your feelings out." Or simply be there and listen. This can be the most nurturing and loving way you can help the healing begin.

Chapter 2:

No Blueprint for Grief

Peace lily: Innocence, peacetime, hope, optimism, healing, sympathy, purity

It's ironic. Death comes to us all, but we all react to death in different ways. When you are grieving, you experience a whole range of emotions. They will likely be confusing and perhaps even frightening. You can easily feel out of control or in the grip of something larger than yourself. It may be hard to grasp, but these feelings—and all the others you may experience—are completely normal.

Despite the fact that most people experience many of the same emotions, it's important to understand that there is no blueprint for grief. Despite what you may have heard, grief doesn't happen in a certain order, in a set of predetermined stages. The process can differ according to whether you're grieving a death, divorce, or another loss.

In this book, I'm going to focus on the grief that results when someone dies.

Whatever you're feeling and in whatever order the feelings happen, they are valid and understandable. Grieving is so very personal; no one can tell you you're doing it wrong. They may try to, but hold fast to the belief that your individual pain is not something that can be dictated by someone else. The grief is your personal reaction to a tragedy.

Your Frame of Reference

Your grief process will begin at a different time and progress at a different speed depending on many factors. The death you're grieving may be that of a family member, friend, or another person who was important to you. It may have been caused by an illness, an accident, or another tragedy. The death may have been very recent, or it may have happened a while ago.

Other factors will influence how your grief unfolds. First, there is your closeness to the person you're grieving. Was the person who died a close family member, or was it a more distant relation you never really got a chance to know well? Was it a dear friend or lover that you shared special, deep feelings with? Was it someone from your wider circle of acquaintances? A coworker who had given you an important experience of support? A young person whom you had seen grow from early childhood? None of these relationships comes with a specific way to grieve or a length of time for the grief to last. The death of someone you haven't seen in years may still cause deep grief as you remember the closeness you shared at one point in your lives.

Your grief may be influenced by factors including your cultural upbringing. If you belong to a large, close-knit extended family, you are likely to have many others around you. Each person will be experiencing grief in their own way, which may not be the same way that you do. If there is someone close to you who shares your experience of grief, the process may be easier for you. But grief is so very personal that, even in that kind of family, you may feel alone, separated, and stranded in your own complicated feelings.

Your religious community can make a difference, too. If you have rituals that surround a death, you may find that they can carry you through the things that need to be done. However, following a routine such as this may only delay the feelings that will eventually well up inside you. Your religion could give you comfort about what awaits your loved one in the afterlife. But it could also fill you with doubt, especially if you have questions about how the religion views death. A ritual may feel strained or impersonal to you when you are going through pain, or it could provide comfort in some measure. If your experience differs from that of other believers, they may not understand your feelings or expressions of grief. But those expressions are not to be discounted, for they are authentic and personal.

Your age may influence the way you grieve. If you are younger and have never experienced the death of someone close, your emotions are likely to be chaotic. You may not understand how you're "supposed" to act and copy what you see other people doing. This can be useful when you are considering the rituals surrounding death—the actions that are expected of you at a funeral or memorial service, for example. But while other people can assist you, they can't know what stage of grieving you're at or how you feel deep inside.

The age of the person who has died can make a difference, too. But be careful of the expectations other people have of you. If the person was old, your relatives may say what a good life the person lived and how they are now out of their pain. This may reflect how they feel, but your feelings may be entirely different. You may regret not spending more time with them or harbor feelings of resentment about how they treated you in the past. Those feelings, too, are valid. There is no one right way to feel.

If, on the other hand, it's a young child who has died from an accident or illness, your relatives may exhibit extreme emotion while you are still numb and disbelieving. That stage of your emotions may last for quite a while. You could easily be out of sync with the feelings of others. This doesn't mean that you have no feelings or are heartless. Only later will your emotions become as extreme as others' were at first.

More Feelings

You may not begin grieving right away. Sometimes it takes a while for the initial shock to wear off and the grief to fully hit you. You could shuffle through what seems like a normal life on a kind of autopilot until the grief hits you unexpectedly. In the last chapter, I explained what some of the emotions associated with grief might be, but there are others.

Confusion

Confusion is one of the most common emotions to feel after a death. You may not know exactly how you're supposed to feel, especially if you're a young person who has less experience with death. Of course, an older person can feel confusion, too. Perhaps some family members' relationship with the person who died was complicated, built on a foundation not of pure love but one that included hurt, abandonment, jealousy, or disagreement. Perhaps your relationship with the deceased was like that.

You may also experience confusion if you're now responsible for dealing with the death of a parent, for example. There will be so many demands on you—notifying relatives, choosing a casket, writing an obituary notice for the newspapers, selecting readings and music for the funeral, and seemingly endless other arrangements. If there is no other person to take on some of the necessities, you can easily be overwhelmed and confused with questions like: What comes next? Have I forgotten something? Should I have done this another way?

Bargaining

Bargaining occurs when you want to make a deal with the forces of the universe, usually God, that would bring the loved one back. It's a deep expression of grief. You may say, "Why did my loved one die? Why couldn't it have been me? I'd do anything to have them back again."

Deep down, you know that this won't happen, but you still express the wish or hope. Friends or family members trying to be logical or talk you out of this phase of grief or way of thinking will not do any good. It's an illogical fantasy that won't respond to rationality. All they can do is offer comfort and say, "I understand. I'm here for you."

Anger

When the death was caused by an accident, murder, or suicide, anger is a common reaction. Your anger can be directed at the loved one who died, the person who caused the accident, or someone who is perceived to be responsible for the death. In the case of a young child who died of illness, for example, you could feel angry with the doctors who weren't able to save them, even if the illness was incurable. Some people even blame God and feel angry that their loved one was taken. Again, logic will not help. Only time and compassionate understanding will help reduce the anger.

Projection

Displaced anger, or projection, occurs when you see something or someone that triggers the deep emotions you have been feeling. It can be as simple as seeing a couple holding hands, reminding you of the love of a spouse who has died. It could be the sight of children playing in a park. You may feel that anyone who is showing pleasure or laughing is being disrespectful of your loved one or your grief. The anger is not really directed at the person or people you see. It's just that the reminder of your pain makes you angry. Since there usually isn't anyone present who really merits the emotion, it's projected onto the person who causes the reminder. You usually don't express this in words but just experience a feeling of profound pain.

Panic

The death may create feelings of insecurity and panic—*How can I ever live without my husband? He took care of everything. I don't know what I'll do without him. I can't face going to the funeral.*

A bereaved person may even wish that they were dead instead of their loved one. As with bargaining and anger, you may experience more irrational thoughts. They will be very real to you, even if others don't understand them. You may experience all the physical signs of panic as well—racing thoughts, rapid heartbeat, shortness of breath, sweaty palms, and others. You may also experience intrusive thoughts at random moments.

Guilt

Another form of irrational, intrusive thoughts is guilt. Even if there is no possible way you were involved in the death, you can still feel guilty simply for being alive when your loved one is dead. It's particularly common in cases when they have died in an accident. *Why wasn't it me? Could I have prevented it? I should have done something. I should have spent more time with them. I didn't say "I love you" the last time I saw her.* These thoughts don't go away quickly. They can persist for months.

Support for the Grieving

A world-renowned psychologist was a guest speaker at a sold-out conference. The atmosphere was electric as the audience waited in anticipation. As the man entered the hall, it became deathly quiet. He walked to the stage and just stood and looked over the audience, not saying a word, just smiling. People in attendance felt there was an aura and presence about this man that was just mesmerizing. You could actually feel it. The longer he stood, the more engaged the audience became. It was as if the healing had commenced, without a word being spoken.

I have never forgotten this powerful revelation. Often during a counseling session, I have stayed silent, even though sometimes it was uncomfortable to do so, just to help a client gather their thoughts or express emotion. It was so effective in helping them get to the root of an issue or deal with their grief. Remember, silence is golden! Your presence is more important than your voice. So, remember this story and say to yourself: "Healing can commence without a word being spoken." If you don't know what to say, or how to say it, just be. A person in need is very intuitive; they will feel your love and empathy without having to hear your voice.

Silence is one of the best gifts you can give to a person who is deep in grief. Your comforting presence is much more important than any words you could say. Especially if you are unsure what to say—which often happens in these situations—sitting with the person wordlessly can help. You may not know how to respond to the irrational thoughts or confused feelings, but wordless gestures like a hug, a pat on the shoulder, an arm around them, or holding their hand can speak volumes.

Remember that everyone grieves differently. Don't assume what your friend or loved one is feeling. You may not understand which stage of grief they are in or what is happening inside their head if they don't speak about it. It's best to avoid the common expressions of solace such as "He's in a better place," or "She's watching over us now." The bereaved may not be focusing on those aspects of death. Instead, they could be feeling anger or guilt and won't be comforted by the typical sayings at all. Above all, it's important not to judge or tell the bereaved person what they should be feeling. In the early days of grief, the person may be feeling numb, but they could also be feeling raw pain.

Physical closeness can convey emotional closeness. If the person says they want to be alone, though, honor that. An intrusive presence is not the same as a comforting one. You can check in on the person after leaving them alone for a time. Calling is less jarring than simply showing up on their doorstep. Even if your friend or loved one turns away, know that they will appreciate the gesture later, when they are less confused about their emotional reactions.

The most important thing is being a comforting, undemanding presence in their life. A gentle, nurturing attitude goes a long way toward helping them heal. Allow time for the initial feelings of pain to resolve before you try to encourage the person to get back out into normal life.

Above all, remember that what you're doing for your friend or loved one is a form of counseling, even if not a professional one. That may, at first, sound overwhelming. You're likely not trained as a counselor. But that doesn't matter. If you listen with comfort and compassion, without judgment, you will be doing the best thing you can possibly do when the grief is still new and raw. So, give them a safe place to be with their feelings. As the initial pain passes, your understanding and loving presence will aid healing.

If you find yourself in this situation, remember what I said in the Introduction: Counseling is a privilege. Helping your loved one is a form of counseling. Being in that relationship with someone you care about is a privilege, too.

Chapter 3:

The Funeral

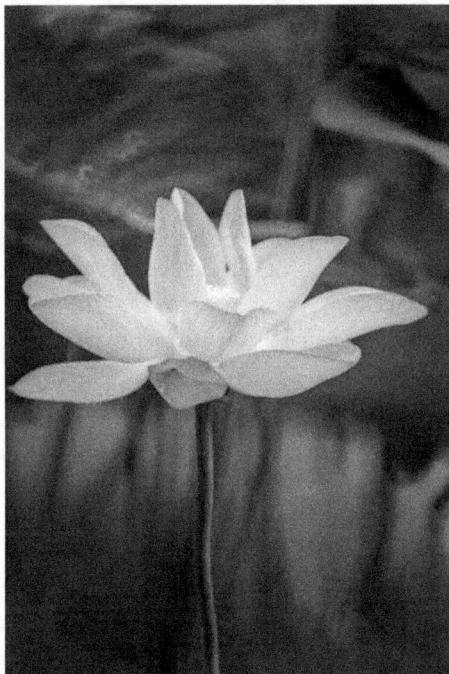

Lotus: Peace, spiritual enlightenment, freedom, calmness, serenity, eternity, purity

Too soon after the death, you'll find yourself caught up in a whirl of decisions to make about the funeral or memorial service. You'll have to do all this before you've even begun coping with the fact that your loved one is gone. In addition to being exhausting, the process will bring up feelings that interfere with all you have to do. Your grief is still fresh, but, to some extent, you have to tamp it down, at least for a while, in order to do what is necessary. If you are the only family member or the only one who lives nearby, your burden is even greater.

Before the Funeral

When a family member dies, you have many duties you must perform and arrangements you need to make. You may not have to make them all alone if there are other family members or trusted friends who can help. But one way or another, these things have to be done.

Immediate Tasks

It's hard to think about, but you must get a pronouncement of the death from the coroner, nursing home, hospice, or hospital, depending on where your loved one died. This document will be necessary for you to get a death certificate, which is not the same thing. A death certificate will be necessary for wrapping up many of your loved one's affairs, such as their financial arrangements. Getting at least 10 certified copies of the death certificate is usually a good idea when it comes to financial matters such as bank accounts and insurance policies that you'll have to deal with later.

Did your loved one make plans for what should happen after their death? Did they leave a will, provide for a funeral plot, name an executor, and leave other important documents? If you're not the named executor, you'll have to get all the documents to the person who is. If the deceased hasn't formalized their wishes, you'll need to talk to other family members and friends to determine if your loved one ever spoke to them about what they wanted done.

One of the many things your loved one may have left instructions about is what they want done with their body. If they have left instructions about a funeral, cremation, or memorial service, it will be easier to carry out these wishes. You'll also want to know whether they've consented to become an organ donor or if they've willed their body to science. If it's been left to your discretion, you'll have to make the decisions.

If there are bereaved children, they will need to stay with family members or neighbors while all these arrangements are being made. Even your loved one's pets will need somewhere to stay, either temporarily or longer if no provisions have been made for them.

Boarding them at a kennel, shelter, or vet may be a possibility for the short term.

One of your most difficult tasks will be notifying family members and friends of the death. Immediate family need to be notified in person or by phone, while close friends and extended family members can receive a call or personal text. Others can be informed in a group text, letter, or on social media, if you feel that's right. Coworkers, religious community members, and other organizations your family member belonged to can help spread the word.

You should also notify your loved one's employer of the death. There are probably arrangements to be made regarding the final check, insurance policies, and other matters such as picking up personal possessions.

Next Steps

Finding your loved one's documents can be vital. In addition to the will, information about bank accounts, deeds, and other financial matters will be necessary. Hopefully, they will have left a ledger or computer file with their accounts and passwords listed, which will make it easier to settle their financial affairs. Their insurance policies will also need to be found.

Memorial and funeral arrangements also need to be made. Who will write the obituary, and will it be published online, in the paper, or both? Your loved one's religious preferences may determine what kind of funeral or memorial service they wanted, but there are still many elements to consider. The biggest one is whether there will be a funeral or cremation. Also, you should determine whether there is to be a visitation before the funeral. After that, there are details that need to be settled about what cemetery will be used and whether your loved one had already made arrangements for this. Similarly, the site of a cremation and whether the ashes will be kept or dispersed need to be determined. Local regulations regarding spreading ashes outdoors should be checked.

Other seemingly small details will add up. Who will select a person, or persons, to give a eulogy? If your loved one belonged to a church, synagogue, or other faith community, who will preside over the service? Will there be a reception afterward, and who will be responsible for securing a location, issuing invitations, and providing the food?

It's terrible to think about, but people's homes are often robbed while the funeral occurs. Someone should be asked to stay at your loved one's house rather than coming to the services. They can also take care of finding and locking up all the valuables like jewelry, cash, or collectibles.

Having your loved one's mail and email forwarded to you or another family member is a detail that is too often forgotten. The mail can also help you determine where they did their banking and what credit cards, loans, and other bills they may have been paying. You may have to reach out to the email provider to determine the requirements for being let into the email account, which can be complicated.

After the Funeral

In the weeks following the death and funeral, there will still be many duties you'll need to perform or delegate. You'll need to make a list of the person's assets and whether the house, car, and other belongings are to be sold or inherited by a particular person. There will be paperwork required no matter what you do. A lawyer, the executor, and perhaps even a mediator may be necessary to clear up the situation.

You will also need to give the will to the executor, if that's not you, and take it to the local probate office. Probate is meant to ensure that any remaining debts are paid and that the beneficiaries receive the remaining assets. You may also want to hire a trusts and estates attorney, especially if the will is complex or you're unfamiliar with the procedures. A CPA can also prepare the person's final tax return and help with taxes on any inheritances. If there is no will, the probate court will use local laws to determine who inherits the assets.

While you're waiting for the estate to be settled, you can pay off remaining bills such as credit cards and then close those accounts. You can also cancel any services your loved one was responsible for, such as cable, Internet, water, and electricity.

Many agencies such as the Social Security Administration, insurance companies, the Department of Motor Vehicles, credit agencies, voter registration office, and perhaps the Department of Veterans Affairs need to be notified of the death.

Don't forget to send thank you notes, too, or delegate that task to another family member. The floral tributes, charitable donations, and other memorials will need to be recognized and your appreciation shown.

Your State of Mind

Your state of mind during the preparations for the future will be complicated. Afterward, you may still be in a state of disbelief, especially if the death has been a sudden one. The pain can be intense since it hasn't had time to ease. You may find yourself fluctuating between being lucid as you make all the arrangements, being in a daze as you go through the motions, and being distraught with all the condolences.

The anguish and confusion you feel can overwhelm you at times. Don't be ashamed if you have a breakdown. It's a normal reaction and completely understandable. Your emotions are what they are, and no one can tell you the proper way to grieve (though some may try to). Get used to the idea that someone else will criticize something that you've done. Everyone will have opinions. Comfort yourself with the knowledge that you are doing the best you can at a very confusing and emotional time.

Pleasant memories can suddenly plunge you into moments of intense sadness as you realize the good times are now gone. Your emotions are on a roller coaster that will continue for some time. While everyone's experience of grief is different, there are certain emotions that you can expect, in some order and at some time.

Stress and Anxiety

With all the decisions you'll make and all the people you'll have to deal with, it's no wonder that you'll be feeling stress. Even after the funeral itself is over, you'll still have to deal with many details that can seem overwhelming. You'll be wanting time to decompress and begin your grieving process, but you may be the one who writes cards thanking people for their donations of flowers or their contributions to charities.

The thought of having friends and relatives who constantly want to check in on you and ask how you're doing can be overwhelming and painful in itself. Wanting to avoid other people is a natural reaction. That may be hard to do, though, especially if you live with others. On the other hand, you may want to take comfort in the presence of people but feel like you've been abandoned. Other people—even friends and family members—may tend to get on with their own lives after a while. You may still need emotional support, and it may seem to disappear just when you would welcome it most.

Many of my clients have been confused and saddened that certain people have not made contact with them. It's important to realize that, just as you may not have known how to act and what to say to others, they may be feeling the same way. Should they show their deep sorrow, or will that only deepen yours? If they don't, will you think they are uncaring? In reality, even people who are close to you may have trouble expressing their emotions. They may be genuinely confused about their own feelings, or they may be trying not to cause you more pain, not realizing that they are doing just that. Your friends and family are likely not being insensitive; they may perhaps be too sensitive of your feelings.

Along with the stress you feel may come anxiety. You could be plagued by doubts. *Did I do everything right? What did the family think of the arrangements I made? Did I remember everything that needed to be done?* And then there's the big question: *What do I do next?*

You may have heard that it's a bad idea to make big decisions or large changes right after a death, but sometimes you're forced into them. You may have to find a new place to live, for example, if you didn't inherit the family home or can't pay the taxes or upkeep on it. Moving always brings with it stress and anxiety, which will only compound that which you already feel. In addition, you may be experiencing irrational thinking, which will make decisions just that much more difficult.

Take Care of Yourself

Alleviating the stress and anxiety you have been feeling is something you should address. Ignoring it only makes it worse. Although it accumulates, you have allies.

Make an appointment with your family doctor, especially if you are having difficulty sleeping. The doctor can analyze whether this is becoming a serious problem and give you advice on how you can restore your sleep pattern to normal. They may even prescribe a sleep aid for short-term use if they feel it's necessary.

Also, leverage the help you have around you. Many friends and relatives who want to help but don't know what to do can be called on for assistance. Don't be afraid to delegate tasks to them. If you have them take excess flowers to the hospital, address envelopes, or wash dishes from the wake or reception and get them back to the people who brought them, they'll be pitching in to take the burden off you. In addition to cooking a hot meal for you, there are many chores someone else can take over. Walking the dog and cleaning up after it will be welcome. Trips to the grocery store for staples that have run low will save you time and trouble. Babysitting, yard work, or driving you to appointments will relieve some of your daily burdens. When someone asks what they can do, give them a specific way to help.

In Chapter 4, I'll be discussing more about how mental health professionals can help you with problems such as sorrow, stress, anxiety, and other confusing emotions. For now, just know that resources are available. Grief therapy is a speciality that many counselors offer. Bereavement therapy groups are often offered at hospitals and hospices. You can Google counselors and groups in your area or find online groups and sites that encourage you to share pictures, memories, poems, and journal entries about your loved one. For example, just type "grief" into the search bar on Facebook and you'll find groups that address everything from grief over the loss of a parent to grief yoga.

Perhaps one of the best resources you can turn to is actually the funeral director you'll deal with. Even after the funeral itself, they can be a great help. They're available 24 hours a day to meet your many needs. In addition to making all the physical arrangements for the event, they are trained in helping people deal with the various ways grief can manifest. Feel free to contact them at any time after the funeral. They may contact you as well, weeks or months after the funeral to check up on you and how you are managing.

Who Can Help?

There are two people who can ease the burden. First is your family doctor. Of course, the doctor will be the one who signs the death certificate, but their assistance doesn't stop there. They can also monitor your medical requirements—for example, your sleep needs. Your GP will assess your state of mind and general well-being. Your discussion with the doctor may include whether you might need antianxiety medication. Don't assume you need medication based on what I say in this book. Only your doctor can make a medical determination. If they do prescribe medication, be sure to take it only as directed. Check in with your doctor if you have side effects and before you stop taking the medication.

Again, another important resource is the funeral director, who has years of training and experience in helping people like you manage the complex arrangements for the funeral. From the purely physical to the emotional repercussions of a death, your funeral director can be your saving grace. They have plenty of expertise in dealing with people who are overwhelmed by the often-daunting requirements as well as the overwhelming feelings following a loss. They are often the first person you contact when a death occurs, and they know what you are feeling and what to do.

The funeral director can assist in many of the arrangements that you may not have thought of, such as sending the obituary to local news outlets and setting up sites for online memorial donations and tributes.

They also know the ins and outs of legal requirements that you don't. They can assist with death certificates and explain the benefits available from the Social Security Administration or the Veterans Benefits Administration.

The services a funeral director can provide to offer comfort are called grief support or aftercare. They also know the things not to say to you in your time of bereavement. Years of experience have taught them the subtleties of using body language and eye contact to make you feel they are attentive to your needs. They create a safe space for you to both make necessary arrangements and express your grief.

Most of all, the funeral director can put you in touch with the other grief-management resources you need. They'll have books and pamphlets that explain the grieving process and information about local bereavement groups and organizations. And they reach out to the family in the weeks and months after the funeral to make sure that their continuing needs are being met. Many people in my practice have described the funeral director as their "saving grace" for all they do before, during, and after the funeral.

Part 2:

Private Exodus From Self

Chapter 4:

The Loneliness

Violet: Purity, healing, peace, humility, innocence, inspiration

The funeral can be an important ceremony, but after all the words have been said, the rituals done, and the people have gone home, what sets in is loneliness. It can manifest as a vague but lingering feeling of absence, but it can also be a profoundly painful storm. It can seem larger than you ever thought you could bear. Or it can be a little voice in the back of your brain, reminding you that your loved one is not coming back.

When everyone else's life seems to be getting back to normal, your reality may feel even more foreign and painful. Your immediate distress may have lessened, but your feelings are likely to be no less profound. You could be absolutely miserable while everyone around you seems to be returning to their everyday lives and routines.

However you experience loneliness, it's important to find ways to move through it and past it eventually. The process will take time and be difficult, but once the loneliness retreats, you'll be in a better emotional space.

Loneliness Descends

You're especially vulnerable to loneliness after the funeral. All your friends and family will have gone home. Maybe one or two will have stayed with you for a night or two, but even they have left. You may have felt stifled by their presence, unable to express the many confused feelings you've been having. You may be weary of having to keep up appearances, pretending that you're really okay. When everyone's gone, you don't have to keep the mask in place anymore.

Or, if you don't live alone, you may be hemmed in by people who are feeling the same things you are. You could feel alone in a group. If you have family who live with you, they may be able to offer some comfort—or maybe not, as they may be tangled up in their own confusion and pain. Roommates may not be much comfort, even if they have suffered a loss, too. Your grief is always different, personal to you. You could feel that no one understands. You're alone in your grief. And that brings on loneliness.

Nighttime is the worst. When you close the door and try to sleep, you're likely to be invaded by memories of your loved one. You may remember the good times you shared when they were alive, or you may imagine what it was like for them to die. But most of all, you feel their absence. In many cases, you go through loneliness on your own. You can't imagine it will ever ease up, and you don't know how to express it to anyone else. Then day dawns, and it's no better.

Learning to Cope

How can you cope with the loneliness and all the other confused and painful feelings you will experience? Once the initial emotions ease up—and they will, fading a little as time blunts their edges—there are things you can do to make the transition to a more settled, peaceful life. For a long time, perhaps, it won't be the life you've known before. It may never be exactly the same. You'll still miss your friend or loved one and feel a twinge when you think of them, but your grief won't be as overwhelming. Peace and healing will begin to return.

Here's an example. Elizabeth called on my counseling services approximately a year before her husband, John, passed away. John had been placed in end-of-life care for three years. They had a very long, loving relationship and marriage. However, Elizabeth's care for John was so intense that she often would lose touch with her own needs, goals, desires, and feelings. She desperately wanted to make John always feel loved and nurtured.

Throughout their marriage, they had a real commitment to each other that didn't involve a huge friendship network. The communities around them were caring, but Elizabeth and John were happy to be two peas in a pod. Their extended family was very important to them, but they were content to just have their own company and that of their children.

I sensed that even though Elizabeth knew John was in decline and she would soon lose him, she was going to have great difficulty moving on with her life. We discussed this. I remarked that it was going to be difficult when John passed as he had been what Elizabeth called "her whole life." John's care and well-being had always been Elizabeth's primary focus.

I advised that she should prepare. Were there classes or groups that she might be interested in joining? Elizabeth took my advice and looked into exercise and yoga classes. She also reconnected with a good friend during this time.

This proved to be her saving grace, to some degree, when John passed away. Elizabeth remembered the conversations we'd had and was grateful that I'd spoken of this. It helped her with creating some routine, physical activity, and friendships.

However, Elizabeth said that the loneliness at night was nearly unbearable, even though her family was very proactive in giving love and support with outings and family gatherings. Elizabeth mentioned the nights and the loneliness were very difficult to bear, mentioning that she was distraught and cried uncontrollably at times.

Even though Elizabeth had time to process the inevitable and had a long and fulfilling life with John, and even though she took steps to fill the inevitable void that was going to come, Elizabeth just missed John desperately. The battle with the transition to life without her husband took time.

Loneliness can be inevitable and extremely painful for many people trying to cope with grief. Undoubtedly, Elizabeth will miss John for the rest of her life. But Elizabeth has progressed emotionally and mentally enough now to be able to live her life again.

What to Do and What to Avoid

Elizabeth learned that there were things she could do to help alleviate her loneliness and misery. You can learn from her experiences how to move beyond the overwhelming feelings and concerns that envelop you. There's a way out of the tunnel of confused emotions and irrational thoughts you've been going through.

The first thing to do is to develop a routine. This will help ground you in familiar activities that will remind you of what your life was like before the death occurred. You can start out slowly by simply making yourself a cup of tea or coffee. The routine motions of getting a cup and starting the coffee maker or choosing a teabag can ground you. When you take your first sip, you can congratulate yourself because you have taken a step toward establishing a daily routine that can carry you through the hard times.

Gradually, you can add other people into your routines. When friends or family members call with invitations to come over or go out for coffee, you can take them up on it. Fresh air is a great restorative. Your friends or family members will know that you're still going through a difficult time, so they shouldn't put too much pressure on you to be too perky and outgoing. Just going out doesn't commit you to a full evening of socialization. You can leave anytime you feel the need to. Your friends will understand if you have to make an excuse and go home. They'll probably even call later to make sure you're okay. Little by little, you'll stretch your social skills and rediscover your ability to interact with others in a nurturing setting.

Or like Elizabeth, you can take up an activity or hobby, especially one that gets you out of the house and gets you moving. Gentle aerobics or tai chi will help get your body in motion again and also allow you to interact with a nonthreatening group of people who don't know what you've been going through. If you don't tell them about the death, they won't be tiptoeing around the subject. Other interests can get you out of the house and into the world as well. A book club, walk-a-thon, swing dance class, fundraising organization, or animal rescue volunteer opportunity may be the right place for you to get back into action.

If you prefer to take up a solitary activity, consider running, jogging, hiking, or swimming. All are good exercise—and exercise is beneficial for both your body and mind. Keeping yourself in good health is important, after all. If you let yourself get rundown, you're more susceptible to not only lowered immunity but also to a return of your low moods. It's best to pay attention to your sleep, diet, and exercise to keep your body running right as your mind begins to settle into a healthful routine.

Getting a pet is also a good idea if you don't already have one. With a dog, you have a built-in routine with feeding, watering, grooming, walking, and cleaning up after them. Animals have the advantage of offering you unconditional love, interaction, and distraction. A puppy, a kitten, even a bird or fish, require your attention and care. Even if you feel you don't care about anything anymore, a pet can bring you back into the life of the living.

If you absolutely can't venture out just yet, use the power of the Internet to make connections. You can send instant messages to your friends and family members. You can join support groups on Facebook or post poems, pictures, or other remembrances of your loved one. People can respond with encouraging messages, remembrances of their own, or simple clicks of like, love, or care that will let you know you are in their thoughts.

However, spending too much time online can be hazardous to your mental health. If you spend too much time brooding and scrolling, you may think you're maintaining contact with the world, but you're really just staying inside yourself and inside your own head with your thoughts. That gets in the way of healing.

If any of these suggestions feel overwhelming right now, at least know that they are out there for you when you are ready for them. It's perfectly okay to let other people know that you're not yet at the point in your healing where you can let them into your grief-filled existence. If necessary, be a little selfish with your time and attention. You need to conserve your mental and emotional energy so you can get through the day. That's okay if that's what's right for you. Don't listen to the people who try to push you into phases of healing before you're ready for them. Healing from grief is very personal and doesn't have to meet other people's expectations.

Your Support System

If you feel you need more support on your healing journey through grief, consider online support systems, including online therapy groups and online therapists. Since the COVID-19 pandemic, more doctors, psychiatrists, and therapists are offering telehealth sessions instead of in-person visits. If you're not yet able to leave your house, consider trying one of these options.

Whether you choose online or in-person help, doctors and therapists are perhaps the most helpful people when it comes to dealing with your changing emotions and feelings you don't understand.

There are many different kinds of mental health workers who can be vital parts of your support system. Therapists, counselors, social workers, marriage and family counselors, group therapists, and trauma counselors are all professionals who can help you. When you're looking for a therapist or counselor, don't be afraid to ask what they specialize in. There are those who specialize in mood disorders like depression and anxiety. Some are even open to grief-specific counseling. Counselors with a religious point of view can be particularly compassionate and understanding.

Compassion and understanding are essential if a counselor is to be successful at helping a person who is in pain. Counselors and therapists use a technique called "active listening" or "attentive listening." With active listening, the counselor listens attentively to what the client is saying. Often the counselor uses silence. Remaining quiet while the client sits with their feelings rather than pushing them to respond to questions can help the person in gathering their thoughts and getting better control of their emotions.

Active listening means being fully present in the conversation and not allowing distractions to get you off-topic. You maintain good eye contact, but without staring directly into the speaker's eyes. Looking to the side or down occasionally or blinking in a natural manner will make the person feel more comfortable.

The counselor uses nonverbal cues to help determine what the client is feeling. For example, if the client has tight muscles and crossed arms, they may be feeling anger or resistance. If the client looks down a lot, they may be uncomfortable with the direction the conversation is taking. That's not a signal that the counselor should ignore the topic, but they may possibly want to back off and come back to it later when the client is more ready to discuss it.

Above all, attentive listening means letting the client guide the content of the session. The therapist may use open-ended questions to avoid directing the client or telling them how they ought to feel. The counselor can also repeat or paraphrase what the client has said in order to make sure they understand the client's feelings. Overall, they listen in order to understand rather than listen to prepare a response. Withholding judgment and not giving advice until the right moment are the essence of attentive listening.

The best therapists make a session feel like they're just having a pleasant chat with the client. It doesn't feel like a therapeutic encounter or a session probing memories and feelings. The therapist doesn't ask many questions or confront the client. You should feel free to say anything, even if you think it expresses a bad side of you or an emotion you're ashamed of feeling.

The therapist should understand your frame of reference, whether you come from a close-knit family or an independent existence. They will understand that everyone grieves differently—there isn't one right way to feel or to heal. Even if you're the sort of person who prefers to go at it alone, finding a therapist or counselor you can work with will truly help you work through your loss and arrive at a better place, with your grief lessened and your coping skills enhanced.

Chapter 5:

Who Am I?

Peony: Peace, hope, honor, prosperity, love

You've experienced one big change in your life, and you're facing another one. You've lived through the death of a loved one, and now you have to learn to live without them. Just when you thought you were through with the cascade of emotions that go with a loved one's death, suddenly, you are faced with a whole new set of feelings.

As you try to adapt to your new circumstances, it's easy to forget who you really are. Your life has changed in so many ways. A presence you were used to has left and taken a part of you with it. Now, you have to pick up the pieces and go on, but you may feel lost, not in touch with the you that was there before. You have to rebuild yourself, and that's hard.

It's good to remind yourself of some of the concepts we've introduced in this book. They'll help in understanding the changes you're going through now.

- **Grief has no timeline.** No one can tell you how long it will take to adjust to the death. Just because one of your friends or family members seems to have moved on doesn't mean that you should have.

- **Grief is a roller coaster.** Your emotions fluctuate unpredictably. You go from thinking you're on an even keel to suddenly feeling out of control. Your emotions can range wildly from deep sorrow to numbness, from calm to agitation.

- **Grief is a complex emotional state.** Grief is not a single thing. It's affected by thoughts and emotions and even your bodily reactions. It is composed of love, sadness, fear of abandonment, nostalgia, despair, and more.

- **Grief affects your behavior.** You may act irrationally. You may sleep too much or too little. You could isolate yourself or need people around you at all times. You may be able to concentrate or be completely scattered.

All the changes you're going through—your emotions, your behavior, your life circumstances—are difficult to navigate through. Life change is hard, and you must be strong to get through it.

Setbacks and Troubleshooting

In the weeks and months following the death of a loved one, you may feel that you are able to go back to your usual social life as it was before. After all, you'll have to eventually. Even if your grief lasts for years, the world outside is waiting for you to re-enter it. Interacting with society once again may not be easy, though. Your first attempts may not be successful. Certain setbacks can keep you from accomplishing your goal of getting back into the world.

First, even though you may think you're ready for the outside world, you may not be. Your mind may be telling you that you can handle social interactions again, but it could be wrong. You may need more time before you try. Of course, making the attempt is good in itself. You can try out small, short interactions with friends. Your attempts at re-entering society can seem harmless—and they are—but there's a chance it won't go well. You may experience an overflow of emotions, perhaps only when you return home.

If this happens, don't give up on the idea entirely. Just wait a while and try again. The next time it could go better. The process isn't easy, but it beats staying cut off and lonely. Eventually, your mindset will change, and you'll be able to handle brief outings at first and then longer ones. Don't jump back into a class reunion right away. Start simply by having a friend over for coffee. Notice whether you feel more comfortable with a friend or with a family member. Let that realization guide you in deciding what social interactions you're ready for.

After a while, it may become uncomfortable or even annoying when your friends and loved ones keep asking you, "How are you doing?" In many cases, you respond with the accepted social response of "fine." But that's not the truth, and it may feel forced.

You have a choice of other, more honest, responses, though. You can say, "It's hard, but I'm starting to do better," or "I'm still feeling upset," or even "I know you mean well, but I'm not able to talk about it yet." You can add, "Thanks for asking. It means a lot to me."

Your strong emotions will persist for some time. Sadness, frustration, hopelessness, and even anger will not go away just because you want to feel better. Repressing them is a way of denying they exist. But they're still there underneath the surface and will erupt when you least expect it. It can be better to let them out in a safe setting. People can mask their true feelings and emotions for many reasons. This harms them and others around them in the long run. Always express emotion—never suppress it.

Once, I went out to an isolated sheep station because I received a phone call from a concerned wife, Angela, about the mental health of her husband, Stephen. The problem was caused not by the death of a loved one but by the death of a dream—his farm.

A severe drought and then devastating floods had decimated their livestock and property. Stephen agreed to see me just to "shut Angela up." As I drove to the homestead, I could see how meticulously cared for and orderly everything around me was, from the machinery to the plants, sheds, and equipment. I took a mental note.

Stephen had a grip like a vise as he shook my hand and a hardened face from years of hard work. However, there was a sadness in his eyes. Stephen's voice and demeanor were conflicted because he had endured so much hardship. Another mental note.

Angela left us in the dining room to talk. Stephen spoke of how he had only 15% of his stock remaining. Only the previous month, he'd gone to a watering point on his property to find 200 sheep dead because of the drought conditions that had made the water undrinkable. There was not a quiver in his voice. Stephen even chuckled about these events as he spoke about them. But he was urgent in his actions.

"Here, I'll show you a video. Check this out." He sounded proud, but the video footage showed years of total devastation of his property.

We went back to the dining table, and I questioned his bravado and demeanor after having endured so much hardship.

Stephen paused, perplexed, and became a little defensive in his body language. I stated how immaculate and meticulously kept everything was around the homestead. Again, after a slight pause, Stephen leaned back in his chair, looked up to the ceiling, and yelled, "Fuck!"

Then he started bawling his eyes out.

I calmly said, "You're safe here mate. Let it out."

Stephen had been masking, or suppressing, his true emotions for years. In part, the masking was irrational behavior. He kept the homestead impeccable so anyone who saw it never questioned how hard his life was. He experienced a great deal of emotional release that day. Over the following months, Stephen made real progress, enabling him to grieve for his loss. We worked on achieving some quality of life after drought and flood.

A month or so after this initial meeting, Angela said how much Stephen had changed. He was no longer so guarded. She thanked me: "You gave my husband back to me."

It may be tempting not to do the strenuous work of re-entering society. You might ask yourself, *Why bother?* Life will go on whether you do or not. That's true, but it will be going on without you and all the things that make you special. If you don't get back into the swing of things, you'll be giving in to loneliness and sorrow. Anxiety and depression are serious conditions that can require medical treatment. Irrational thoughts and behaviors will have a chance to take hold.

If you find returning to life and recreating yourself too difficult, ask yourself what the alternative is. The answer: a life in misery that seems to go on and on. Why wouldn't you want to find a way out of that? Releasing your emotions by talking to your friends and relatives, doctor, and funeral director, if you're able to, gives you options. In Chapters 3 and 4, I've talked about how you can find help for your confused emotions and irrational behaviors. Now, I'll delve more into medical solutions.

Medicine and Therapy

Everyone's timeline for grief is different, but there's a point where anxiety and depression turn into real problems. Both can become serious medical conditions. Anxiety disorders and major depressive disorders can be long-lasting and dangerous. If you don't take care of them promptly, you're letting yourself in for troublesome emotions that last longer than they have to. Fortunately, though, these conditions are treatable. You don't have to be stuck in an anxious and depressed state indefinitely. Reach out for help when you feel the need. Your friends and loved ones can help by telling you when they think you need it. People who are close to you can notice when you are acting erratically or speaking irrationally. They can help you make the decision to go for help.

Depression is particularly serious! Medication may be one aspect of treatment, but the issues that lead you to depression will still be there. With medication, your emotions may now be easier to deal with, but psychotherapy by a professional will address the issues that lead to your depression in the first place.

If you're reluctant to take medication, that's understandable. Psychiatric medications can lead to addiction if they're not prescribed and taken properly. But they can have tremendously positive effects. Antidepressants act to increase chemicals that the brain produces called "neurotransmitters," such as serotonin, dopamine, and norepinephrine. These neurotransmitters lift your mood. You don't get high, but you definitely feel better—less depressed, more energetic, and more hopeful. It usually takes a while for antidepressants to start working, so give them some time before you give up on them.

Your doctor can also prescribe antianxiety medications if you're feeling unsettled and jittery. These meds calm your nerves and even out your reactions. If you've been jumping at the slightest sound or feeling symptoms of anxiety such as a racing heart, sweaty palms, and shaking hands, medication could be one answer. Depending on how severe your symptoms are, the doctor may advise you to take antianxiety meds on a regular schedule or only as needed.

The other medication that your doctor may prescribe is a sleep aid. If you haven't been sleeping for several nights in a row, you could need this kind of help. Lack of sleep isn't good for the body or mind. Sleep aids must be monitored closely by your doctor, who'll tell you how much and for how long to take them. It's important to never take sleep-aid medication in combination with alcohol; this can be very dangerous.

One of my clients needed both therapy and medical support for his condition. About 15 years ago, I had a call from a farmer, Jack. He had just been prescribed antidepressant medication by his doctor, who advised him to make a therapy appointment with me. Jack was hesitant and skeptical at first.

"I don't know if you are going to be able to help me," he said. "I think this is all bullshit anyway."

I asked Jack, "Why do you think this is bullshit?"

Defensively, he blurted, "People that need counseling are just weak."

"You're entitled to your opinion," I replied. "We'll just have coffee then, but I would love to hear how your farm is going, mate."

Jack paused, then abruptly stated, "It's fucking shit."

We continued talking, and an hour and a half later, we were scheduling another appointment. As with many clients, Jack was unaware we'd even been conducting a counseling session. To him, it felt just like a chat.

During the next four months, Jack kept in contact with his doctor, and one time, there was a medication change that helped him achieve a more positive emotional state. Our conversations progressed, and Jack was able to overcome his depression. Four years after that initial appointment, Jack sent me a handwritten letter on the back of an old envelope. It stated, "If it wasn't for you, I would not be here today." I have kept that letter ever since.

Chapter 6:

Rejoice in the Glimmers

Chamomile: Calming properties, tranquility, peace, harmony

No doubt you've heard of triggers. They're words or images that evoke a strong reaction in the person who hears or sees them. At times, triggers are so strong that they can make the person relive the emotions they felt when the original incident happened. A trigger can even cause a panic attack or a meltdown if the original incident was particularly traumatic, like a rape or physical abuse.

The concept of triggers has become controversial. Some people— those who have never experienced them—don't believe that triggers exist or realize the emotional trauma they can cause as a person relives the event. These are the people who believe that traumas are something you can and should just get over.

Unfortunately, some of these people also believe that grief is something you should just get over in a short amount of time. If they've never experienced a traumatic death themselves, they may not realize the depths of grief or the fact that everyone grieves in their own way, in their own time.

Wouldn't it be great, though, if there were something that was the opposite of a trigger? Well, there is—a glimmer!

What Are Glimmers?

Glimmers are small glimpses of hope, peace, or joy that you notice despite still being in one of the stages of grief. As the word "glimmer" suggests, they don't have to last for a long time. They don't erase grief. They just give you a little break from it. You have a chance to catch your breath, to glimpse the possibility of healing, and to find a moment of peace. Embracing these moments will help your nervous system prepare for change and a growing mindset of comfort and peace.

Glimmers appear when you're ready to notice them. They happen when you've reached a point in your journey where you're able to let in a ray of light. You'll observe glimmers in quiet moments of reflection. They can happen anywhere that touches something deep inside you. A glimmer may remind you of an experience you shared with a loved one or something you think they would have enjoyed. They are little windows into a happier time in the past or a better time to come.

You can find glimmers in nature and the environment. That's one of the most common places to experience them. But you can also find glimmers at home—a dog wagging its tail or a kitten purring, a baby's laugh, a flowering plant on the windowsill, the smell of your favorite tea brewing, or the chime of a grandfather clock. You can recognize glimmers with your senses when you feel the wind or rain against your skin, see sunlight filtering through the leaves, or hear the music from an ice-cream truck. If your mind is open to glimmers, they will appear when you least expect them.

Approximately six months after my wife passed, I experienced a glimmer. There was a beautiful beach with a jetty where I often strolled each morning, though I was oblivious to my surroundings. I was suffering from depression, but I was on medication for it and receiving psychotherapy. I felt disillusioned by certain aspects of my recovery.

I walked to try and clear my head and become lost in my thoughts. Often, I wasn't even aware of where I had walked that morning when I arrived back home. One day, on a beautiful summer morning, I took a different route than usual. I went out through the eucalyptus trees that wound alongside a rarely used dirt track. Suddenly, I noticed young birds squawking in the tree above me, urgently wanting their mother to feed them.

I stopped and watched, thinking to myself, *Those young birds are old enough to find their own food.* I smiled and watched them for about 10 minutes. Off the mother bird went, returning a little later with a full beak. The babies' wings started flapping. They were squabbling to get the best vantage point for the next mouthful. I just started laughing at this commotion—this beautiful sight.

I walked on and came to a creek just off the track and sat down on the sandbank. Little fish were darting around, mesmerizing me. The sun beat warmly on my back that morning. The salty air was delightful as I drew in deep breaths.

Everything changed for me that day! Yes, there were still going to be difficult times ahead. But I never forgot that moment and that mind shift on that morning; I can picture it like it was yesterday. I can hear all the sounds; I still smell everything so vividly. I rejoiced in the glimmers.

As time passes, you will not only remember this change, but you will also gain amazing insight from the experience. Today, when I have difficulty with life issues, I can remember my glimmers and experience an automatic switch, a change in my mindset. I am grateful for and appreciate what I have. I can smile and see what is beautiful around me.

In my counseling experience, most of my clients have experienced glimmers. When you do, you'll never forget them. They're a way for the mind to shift for just a moment into a different reality. They're a sign that your nervous system is now ready for other emotions to begin filling you.

Glimmers gain power when you acknowledge these moments and voice them. Talking about them—to yourself or to another person—reinforces the experience and makes it more real for you. It makes it easier to look for that specific glimmer again or to encounter new ones.

You'll be looking for the motion of a squirrel in the trees or the scent of a barbecue grill. Each time you notice a different bird and hear its call, you'll remember that your mindset and your emotions are beginning to change.

Emotional Conflict

It's true that when you experience a glimmer, especially for the first time, you may experience an uncomfortable reaction. Perhaps it seems wrong to you that you noticed a moment of joy. After all, you're still dealing with the grief that follows the death of a family member or loved one. You may feel guilt or even anger at yourself for leaving the path of grief to find yourself enjoying something again. You may think that it's disrespectful to your loved one to feel anything but sorrow.

Don't beat yourself up, though. Remember that grief is personal and doesn't run on a specific timeline. You know that it will be broken up by various emotional states—numbness, sorrow, rage, depression, and other feelings. A glimmer is an indication that the course of your grief has entered a new phase. You're not abandoning the sorrow that you naturally still feel and becoming suddenly jolly and uncaring. You're simply allowing in a ray of light.

This is a natural variation in the path of grief. Recognizing a glimmer is a first, small signal that your grief will not last forever, even though at first you might have thought it would. The highs and lows of grief trigger confusing levels of emotion. You may feel unsettled, like you're out of control. In reality, though, your mind and emotions are undergoing a perfectly natural shift. Your brain actually wants more glimmers at this point. You are ready for them.

You'll find that there are certain things that can interfere with your ability to notice and take comfort from glimmers. At first, you may not be far enough along with working through your grief. You heal gradually and can't rush the process. It's just not possible to force yourself to find or notice a glimmer. They occur when you least expect them. You may not be in a mindset where glimmers can get through. You need to switch off your conscious mind and allow your feelings to be activated. A glimmer has to be able to get through all the noise that your mind puts out. When you switch off, you will be able to enjoy the soothing experience you have created for yourself, and glimmers can get in.

Experiencing glimmers works best if you're in a calm and peaceful environment. You're more likely to get the full benefit of them if you're hiking in a lovely natural setting than if you're walking along a busy city street filled with rushing pedestrians and noisy traffic.

It's also possible that you're trying too hard. Glimmers occur when you're not consciously searching for them. They simply appear, coming into your consciousness when you least expect them. That's part of the joy and magic of glimmers—the unexpectedness of them, the inexplicable lift you get from them, the momentary glimpse of the possibility of relief from your feelings of grief.

You'll feel like you're on an emotional roller coaster for a while—seeing a glimmer, then falling back into guilt or sorrow. You might return from a walk where you noticed and appreciated a spring wildflower, then find yourself preparing a lunch for one and be instantly plunged back into grief. You could even revert to your original feelings of grief, sobbing uncontrollably, unable to sleep at night. You may feel you're back to square one.

That's not true, though. You're still on the path toward healing. The glimmer has triggered your mental and emotional systems, and you are now open to more. You will still experience setbacks, but you are coming nearer and nearer to healing. The jolt of experiencing a glimmer has jump-started your emotional reactions. You just need to be on the lookout for more and more. Once you've started noticing them, you're open to glimmers and will begin to notice them more and more. The alternative is to collapse back into the early stages of grief and let the confusion consume you, which will only prolong your feelings of devastation and loss.

In fact, if you take the path of grief, you can experience a psychological condition known as "complicated grief" or "prolonged grief disorder." I'll cover this more in the third book in this series, but for now I'll pass along some basic information. Prolonged grief disorder occurs when you don't make any progress along the path of healing. You get stuck in your negative emotions, and they don't lessen with time. Of course, grief has no timeline. Everyone experiences it differently. But if your grief continues for a long period—more than six months to a year, for example—and it interferes with your daily life, you may be experiencing a psychological disorder.

In addition to the general feelings that anyone with grief experiences, if you have complicated grief, you may feel bitter or numb, or you may not trust other people. Other warning signs include interference with handling your daily routines or wishing you had died with or instead of your loved one.

You're more likely to experience prolonged grief if you've experienced the death of a child or if you already have an underlying condition such as major depressive disorder. You should contact your doctor or a mental health professional if this goes on for a year or if you feel like committing suicide.

A short-term treatment called prolonged grief disorder therapy may help. It's based on psychological and social functioning research. Elements of cognitive behavioral therapy (CBT) are another possibility.

Reflection

What will help you in reaching this new state of mind? Determine this by taking some time off for reflection. You'll be ready to examine yourself when you're at a good point in building up your mental strength with the awareness of glimmers. Selecting a time when you are at a higher point on the roller coaster will help you turn your awareness inward.

Grief wears you out physically and mentally. Taking a break from it is not just necessary—it's inevitable. There will be days when you can simply no longer face your feelings. Seize those moments. Clear away all the emotional clutter such as writing thank-you notes or thinking about who should receive personal mementos from your loved one's belongings. Taking time for reflection can shift your point of view.

One thing to consider is what has worked to help you through your journey and what hasn't. Maybe you rushed into seeing friends too soon. Perhaps you tried too hard to tell yourself that you were really okay. On the other hand, you may have taken your time and been realistic about what you were ready to do. You allowed the first pangs of grief to pass before you set about rebuilding your emotional life into a new normal.

On the other hand, it isn't necessary for you to have all the answers. It's simply too soon to have everything worked out, and if you try, you will risk taking a dive back down the roller coaster to the depths. What you need most of all is some quiet time to yourself so you can listen to your inner voice.

Your inner voice is the part of you that speaks to you when you are still and quiet. Many people think of their inner voice as their conscience, but it's more than that. It's made up of your thoughts and beliefs about yourself and your place in the world. Usually buried in your subconscious, your inner voice will rise to the surface as you take time to reflect. The inner voice is also called self-talk, the messages you send yourself from deep within you. You may have self-talk that says discouraging things like "I'm unlovable" or positive ones like "I deserve happiness." When you engage in reflection, you bring your self-talk to the surface where you can examine it and start to change it if necessary. It is vital for emotional awareness.

Emotional awareness is one of your biggest strengths in making your reflection productive. It's not only being in touch with how you're feeling, though, of course, it's that, too. Emotional awareness means understanding the cycle of emotions. Your thoughts affect your feelings, and your feelings determine your behavior. Thus, if you think you will never get over your feelings of grief, your feelings will continue to be confused and irrational. Then, in turn, those feelings mean that you will refrain from doing things that will help you heal. Your thoughts will be self-fulfilling.

On the other hand, if you think you are on the road to healing, you will have thoughts of hope and peace. Your actions will include looking for glimmers and trying to renew contact with friends and family members. These thoughts will be self-fulfilling, too, but in a good way.

Your Own Best Friend

In reaching increasing levels of healing, you are the best friend you could possibly have. Of course, sympathetic, understanding friends can help, but since the healing occurs inside you, you have the most influence on it. Your loved ones assist in your journey back to peace and emotional balance, but really, you are the one who does the real work and creates spaces where you can make progress.

In a very real sense, you create the environment where you can make progress toward healing. You find the times and spaces where glimmers can be found. You find the time and mental space for moments of reflection that guide you on your journey. In your own time and space, you create clarity for yourself. You approach a kind of emotional balance.

You also discover environments in which you can find peace and healing. It may be a comfortable space in your home where you aren't interrupted by outside noises. It could be a nearby park with a fountain and benches where you can rest peacefully. It could be a time instead of a place—a quiet hour before bedtime that you can share with a pet or an early morning when the sun is just coming up.

The most difficult part of the process may be learning to love yourself again. When you are comfortable with yourself and your spirit is calm, you can let go of the guilt, blame, and emptiness you may have felt. When you love yourself, your mind is capable of shifting into a new space, opening to the possibility of a new life where you are not consumed by grief but able to sit with your sadness in an attitude of possibility.

Part 3:

Reclaimed Life

Chapter 7:

Awakening

Pincushion: Love, purity, peace

At some point in your journey from grief to healing, you will experience an awakening. It's an important moment that indicates that you're starting to come back to life at the same time that you find comfort after your friend or family member's death. It won't be a blinding flash that strikes you all at once. Instead, it will creep up on you, surprising you when you least expect it.

You can expect the glimmers I discussed in the last chapter to continue. At this point, you'll have regained a little energy. Your sensory perception will have been heightened. This can be a wonderful feeling due to the distressing times you have experienced since the passing of your loved one.

But there will also still be twinges of negative feelings that haven't quite disappeared yet. As the feelings of grief begin to mellow out and ease off, you will be able to see that the moments of hope and even joy will become more prominent, easing you into your new life. You won't forget your loved one, of course, and your feelings will remain complicated, but you will feel yourself beginning to awaken to new possibilities.

Moments of Joy and Sorrow

You've been having glimmer moments throughout your life, even if you haven't recognized them as such. The flickering flames of a warming fireplace or a fall bonfire, or even a summer cookout, may have awakened you to the joy of time spent with family. The smell of the pages of a well-loved book or a cup of orange spice tea can stay with you long after the moment has passed. The soft fur and purr of a cat nestled on your lap or the dirt under your fingernails as you plant bulbs that will blossom in the spring are important examples of the sense of touch. Listening to a favorite sonata or hearing popcorn popping can evoke pleasant memories. And the taste of cream cheese icing on a carrot cake or the hoppy flavor of a can of beer can bring back memories of good times.

All these sensations can simply pass you by as you go through life, but they can also stand out as moments that catch your attention, build memories, and bring you joy every time they recur.

If any of these sensory moments are associated with your memories of a friend or loved one who has died—a bonfire you attended together, a sonata you shared at a chamber music concert, or another pleasurable event—the sensation you feel will be even more significant. You may even feel the presence of your loved one with you. It's a profound moment that can awaken you to the possibility of joy even though they have left you.

Then, there are certain events and sensations that will plunge you back into where you began on your journey through grief. For example, you might receive a letter that was addressed to your loved one, or you might find a document in your loved one's handwriting. A creation that your loved one made or a trip to an amusement park can be especially painful if a child is the person you've lost. Voice recordings and videos are particularly powerful. And, of course, family or other gatherings that your loved one enjoyed, like family or class reunions, holiday dinners, important religious observances, and so on, can bring back memories so strongly that you can't help feeling your grief acutely. The sight of an empty chair at the family dinner table is something that will be a heart-rending reminder that your loved one is gone.

You may feel confused about your feelings and how they change from day to day and even hour to hour. You long for more sensory glimmers, but at the same time feel grief, guilt, or even anger because your loved one is not there to share the experience with you. The hints of healing and the hits of grief may happen in rapid succession. You could return from a relaxing walk or drive feeling invigorated and then suddenly collapse in tears when you find yourself preparing your dinner for one.

Your feelings can even be a mixture of both joy and grief at the same time. When you feel a mixture of these emotions, it's confusing. It's hard to hold both in your head at the same time. Instead, your thoughts become a mash-up of confusing feelings—healing and peace combined with sorrow and angst simultaneously. It's a difficult combination for your heart and brain to process.

Grief and Relief

It's important to remember that grief is not linear. As time passes, it will come and go rather than be the constant, excruciating pain that happens when the death has just occurred. The same is true of relief. Your feelings won't go up in a straight line from the depths of sorrow to the plateau of relative calm to the comfort of acceptance. The journey will be messy, consisting of encouraging lifts and crashing lows coming unpredictably. It will be frustrating never knowing what emotion will come next or how long it will last.

Your moment of awakening will come after emotional setbacks, when you need help moving forward. It's very common for the process to happen this way. In fact, 75% of the clients who come to me for grief therapy have reached this stage of the healing process. You'll have been experiencing setbacks and need help moving forward. It may not feel like healing because you're confused and upset with your state of mind and why you're having all these setbacks.

You may feel that you have retreated to the early days of your grief, but that isn't so. All the healing that you have done hasn't simply disappeared. It's just that certain stimuli trigger the negative emotions, just as other sensations trigger positive ones. It's all a part of the process.

As confusing as these highs and lows are, they are actually signs that your emotions are ready for a significant shift. Your mind is becoming capable of holding multiple emotions at the same time, or at least within a short time of each other. Don't be discouraged because some of them are dark, like loneliness or guilt. Just like hope and encouragement, they are part of the process you are going through that will ultimately heal you.

When you've worked through the early stages of grief and have found yourself open to noticing glimmers, you are ready for a revelation. Your mind has gained strength. That increases the frequency and intensity of the signs of progress around you.

The Moment of Awakening

You're beginning to experience some glimmers. This means that you've acquired some emotional control and awareness. You're trying to reinvent yourself. And you've learned to recognize, enjoy, and even anticipate glimmers. You look forward to more of them appearing as you go about your daily rounds.

Suddenly, the setbacks start. You may experience a trigger that evokes them. It could be any reminder of your loved one—a place they loved, a movie you enjoyed together, a diner you used to frequent, a tree they planted, or an old letter they wrote to you. Suddenly, you're plunged back into pain and grief. The negative emotional reaction threatens to derail you from your progress.

You can feel fed up with your negative state of mind and your renewed sense of grief. After all, you were well along your path to renewal, and now you seem to be back where you started. You could be irrationally angry at the person who died for causing you all this pain. You're likely to feel frustrated because of all you've been through and how healing seems further away than ever. You may blame your loved one for causing the setbacks that bring you so much pain.

However, when you experience this confusion of emotions, it's a sign that your brain has been triggered and is ready for a revelation. In fact, it's the key moment for you to experience a profound change in your feelings. This sense that something new is about to unfold is not something that can be taught. It simply unfolds one day, reshaping your understanding of your loved one's death.

Remember that feeling must precede healing. Until you have gone through all the phases—including the emotional setbacks that arise—you will not yet be ready for your emotional wounds to heal. You have to go through the entire journey before you're capable of experiencing the renewal that healing brings. When that moment happens, that revelation will appear spontaneously.

The feelings of joy and hope change your mindset. They prepare it to shift into a different realm, one where positive feelings are at last able to grow and flourish.

At this point, there are two pathways you can follow. One is through confusion and hurt. You can continue to experience sorrow and despair. They will be so familiar to you at this point that you could be reluctant to let go of them. You may feel that moving on from the pain will be a betrayal of your loved one. Fiction is full of depictions of grieving people who never get over it and become bitter and angry.

Healing really isn't a betrayal. It's a natural part of how you adapt to a sad event. It's not about getting over it or getting past it. What you're doing is integrating your loss into your mindset but leaving room for joy to take root as well. How long it will take for this to happen, no one can say. And at first, you may not be able to believe that it ever will.

Then, one day—and it may be on a day when you have hit a rough patch in your healing, one where you feel mired in grief—your mind suddenly switches on and says, "No more!" You may even find yourself saying those exact words.

I've seen this happen often with my own clients. I've even experienced it myself. When you reach the point in your journey when you have at last encountered and enjoyed glimmers and perhaps even fallen back into despair, you hear a voice within you saying, "Do you believe that your loved one would want their legacy to be your continuous misery and sorrow?"

If you have reached this turning point, you have come to a revelation, a shift in your emotions—even a jolt in your perception of grief and healing. Your thoughts of hopelessness and defeat change into hope for the future and even optimism. You'll begin to believe that you can recover from your loss. You really will be okay.

In my grief-counseling practice, I have introduced clients to this concept many times. When a client of mine is stuck, unable to move beyond the setbacks and into the light, I look for exactly the right moment to share it with them. When I do and they finally have this light bulb moment, I notice a change in their body language and facial expression and hear a new note in their voice as well. It's a breakthrough for the client and a profound, nearly overwhelming moment for me as well. Even as a mental health worker, I am nearly overwhelmed by the client's reaction. The change in their perception of healing and comprehension of their ability to experience this awakening is so profound.

The statement I use is not just a message of hope and healing, though of course it is that, too. It's a reflection of the client's readiness for a spiritual awakening that will change their life into a better, more balanced one. They'll never exactly recover from the death as the knowledge of it will always be there. But they will reach a place where they can live with the emotions caused by the loss without having those feelings consume every moment of their lives.

It truly is an awakening of all your senses and your mind and emotions. You'll never forget the moment when it comes upon you. At last, you'll be ready to move into the next phase of your life. You'll never forget your loved one, but you'll be at peace. So, use this exact statement when you need to: "Do you believe your loved one would want their legacy to be your continuous misery and sorrow?" Then watch what it does to your mental and emotional perception.

It truly is astounding how this new comprehension can cause such a profound transition in your life. It was all about timing; the time is right for you to evolve past grief.

The glimmers will come more frequently until they're a part of your everyday life. The setbacks will become fewer and fewer. Your heart will be well on the way to being healed, and you'll be able to welcome a new you into the world.

Chapter 8:

Redefining Yourself

White rose: Pure love, calmness, affection

It's hard to make changes, especially when it comes to remaking your own life. Grief has devastating effects, and it takes real work to put yourself back together again. You've started down that path and learned a lot along the way, but there is still more to experience.

Perhaps the work you've been doing in rebuilding yourself has not gone exactly smoothly. You know that getting past grief is a process that can't be rushed and will present you with setbacks. You may even have lost your sense of identity to a certain extent. Who are you, really? You'll realize your life has been changing, mostly for the better now, but not without trauma along the way.

It's time to take a look at both how the healing process has changed you and how you can continue along the path. It'll be a bumpy one, but you can look back on how far you've come as you journey toward the future. Expect that it will feel like two steps forward and one step back—but notice that the net effect is moving forward!

How You Got Here

Speaking of steps, there are a lot that got you where you are today. You'll have tried any number of techniques that have helped. Here are just a few.

You may have tried getting professional help. A therapist or a grief counselor may have helped you process your feelings. They are specially trained to gently guide you on your passage through grief. Importantly, you'll have had the opportunity to express your emotions without judgment. Your therapist or counselor may have used a number of techniques, most of which come under the general heading of "talk therapy." The most important thing they do is listen as you describe your feelings and what you do about them. They help you develop coping mechanisms to deal with the symptoms of distress you may be feeling. Whether they approach loss and grief from a philosophy of faith-based counseling, psychotherapy, or directive counseling, they can help you get past the hard parts and to a space where you can heal.

Medical doctors are another resource you may have tried. They can evaluate you when you're first bereaved to see if you're physically and mentally okay. You may have had difficulty sleeping, for example, which your family doctor is qualified to help you with. Other physical symptoms you may have experienced, such as high blood pressure, migraines, and other stress responses, are conditions that your doctor can monitor and treat.

Your doctor or a psychiatrist may have prescribed you medications that enable you to sleep and combat the effects of anxiety and depression that often accompany a significant loss. Medication isn't a long-term solution, but with careful monitoring from a professional, it can get you through some of the more devastating feelings that you have experienced.

Your family and friends will have also provided you with the best they could. This may have involved simply listening to you as you talked about your feelings and memories. They may have held your hand when you needed it and encouraged you to go out when you were ready to do that. Because they know you so well, they have most likely been some of your strongest supporters.

It's a truism that time heals wounds, and in this case, time will have had a significant effect on your healing from grief. The further in time you get from the death, the more grief recedes. You don't forget your loved one or the pain you felt, but it definitely becomes easier to bear. You'll have had time from your own frame of reference to process what has happened.

You've also experienced "glimmers"—moments of joy that have come to you through your senses. These brief impressions of sensory delight lift your mood. Often found outside or in nature, they are signals that indicate you are beginning to heal. The capacity for joy and peace reset your emotions to leave you more open to positive feelings.

In addition to these positive feelings, though, you will have had to battle with negative emotions that arose. Perhaps you've felt guilty about feeling momentary relief from your sorrow and grief. Maybe you've been illogically angry that you have let go of your feelings of sadness—that you have abandoned the memories of your loved one or that your emotions have ceased to be as strong. These negative emotions will not be as severe as they once were, but they can still break through at times. Fighting against them has been an important part of healing.

At last, you will have experienced a feeling of awakening from your grief. When this happens, you realize that your loved one would not have wanted you to remain in pain and sorrow for the rest of your life. A close friend, family member, or other loved one would have wanted you to heal and return to feelings of love, fond remembrance, and peace. Lifelong grief is not to be their legacy. Your loved one wouldn't want you to live that way.

All these supports and phases have been vital to moving out of your fog of grief and misery. And they're essential to redefining yourself as a living person, still mindful of the absence of your loved one but not consumed by the enormity of their death. It's time to start living again!

Of course, living with grief will have changed you. You've been through a profound experience that has brought you new insight into the enormity of death and the necessity of continuing to live your best life. But how do you begin to carry on with your life? No doubt, grief has drained you and used up many of your emotional resources. Most of all, it may have sapped your confidence in your ability to go on without your loved one. But you still have that power within you. It's just a matter of tapping into your inner confidence and allowing it to flourish anew.

How can you do that? There are many ways. They do require a little effort, but you'll now have the strength to take on the task ahead of you.

New Confidence

First, you must be aware of the sensory change you'll have undergone. It has been a profound one that has taken you from the physical and mental effects of grief to the beginnings of a new life. That new life will always contain the memories of your loved one, but it will also contain the capacity for healing and peace.

At this point, the fog that enveloped you has lifted, and you have become aware of the moments of beauty that enrich your life. But after so long a time trapped in the fog, how do you re-enter the land of the living? It takes confidence, a quality you may feel you lack after all you've been through.

Whether the clearing of the fog surrounding you has been a mere glimpse of the possibilities beyond sorrow or a revelation of the beauty of the world beyond grief, the relief you'll feel is a force for positive change. If you're able to rejoice in this feeling, you will gain momentum to embrace that change.

Perhaps you have tried before to embrace a new version of your life and been unsuccessful. That doesn't mean you aren't capable of it. It just means the time wasn't right. You still had work to do in facing your grief and moving beyond it. Now, you have enough distance to really make the changes you need to re-enter the world.

One resource you will need is confidence, and yours may have been lost on your journey from grief to healing. The confusion of emotions might have led you to believe that you were weak, unable to deal with life and the world outside. Now that you're feeling better, it's time to uncover the confidence you once had and renew it.

You may have tried to re-enter the world as you journeyed, and you may not have had much luck doing it. It's likely that you simply weren't ready yet. Now is the time to try again. Now you have built up your reserves and are more ready for the world outside. It's time to rebuild your confidence and experience the new you and the world beyond grief.

Think about the things you may have tried to distract yourself from grief. Maybe they didn't work. Maybe you just weren't ready for them to work. Your walks in the woods ended with you feeling desolate. Your attempts to read didn't work because you simply couldn't focus. Your desire to do volunteer work failed to happen because you didn't have the energy to leave your house. You found yourself skipping coffee dates with friends and relatives. No matter what you tried, it didn't work.

Now's your chance to try again. Take some of the things you did in hopes of bringing yourself out of your negative feelings and back into the light, then gather up your courage and plunge back in.

For example, if you've found that being in nature has helped you refresh your spirit, you might want to take up gardening. Getting outside and digging in the dirt is restorative. The feeling of the dirt beneath your fingers and the sight of crocuses coming up in the spring connect you with the earth and growth. If you have a yard, you could begin by cleaning up this space that you've neglected for months. Prune trees and shrubs, feed and water your lawn, rake the leaves— whatever needs doing.

If you live in an apartment, you can still bring the outdoors in. Buy some green plants or indoor flowers to brighten up your surroundings. Select attractive pots that will harmonize with your decor. Green plants and flowers are pleasing to the eyes and to your other senses. You might start small with a selection of herbs growing on your windowsill to use for taking up cooking again.

Cooking will nourish your body as well as your spirit. While you've been suffering, you may have neglected eating well. Your appetite could have been off, or you may not have had the wherewithal to prepare full meals. You may have been living off of fast food and junk food because it's simply easier. That can debilitate you physically. The scent and taste of homemade food are restorative to both the body and soul. They sustain the spirit as well as physical health.

Technology may have progressed while you were lost in grief. Maybe it's time for you to freshen your skills on the latest software. It doesn't have to be a solitary pursuit, either. There are computer classes you can take at your area's adult education program. Through your local school system, you may even be able to find one that's taught by students.

If your computer skills are still current, you might want to consider using your word processor to take up writing. You can write about the friend or loved one you lost, of course, or your journey toward healing. But you can also stretch your wings and write about another topic that has interested you—reflections on nature, the cute things your pets do, poetry about the state of the world, personal essays chronicling your life, memoirs of your family's stories—anything you can think of. You'll find your creative impulses awakening anew.

Volunteer work is another project you can take on, and there are lots of programs that will welcome your help. If you're not ready to jump into full-time volunteer opportunities like food banks, you could help prepare and serve a holiday meal for the homeless. Another excellent opportunity is working at an animal rescue organization. Cats and dogs need care and can lift your spirits at the same time. Or if you're more comfortable staying at home but still want to contribute, you could crochet toys and knit blankets to donate to the local hospital.

The important thing is that you get involved with life again. What you do matters less than the fact that you are doing something. And you don't have to totally change your life. In fact, it's probably better if you pick up some activity that you've neglected while you were struggling. Don't think you have to commit yourself to a project that takes up most of your time. You can try out different opportunities and experiment until you find what's most satisfying to you.

Whatever you choose for your confidence-building activity, make sure that it's not a huge, sweeping change for you. Pursuing an interest you already have in a new or more intense way is probably best. For example, develop an interest such as woodworking into a side gig rather than quitting your day job to make it your new career. Of course, after some time, you may decide that woodworking is your full-time passion, but don't jump into it too quickly.

You've no doubt heard advice not to make big changes after a death, and that's true. Moving to another state or changing careers is likely to be an irrational reaction to having new enthusiasms. In this case, smaller steps are preferable.

Embracing Change

Here's a way to think about embracing change—I've used it many times in my own practice.

First, think of yourself as an apple. You were once ripe and sweet, sitting in the fruit bowl along with the other apples. As the days passed, you changed. You didn't quite look like the other apples anymore. You became a bit softer. Eventually, you were beset with blemishes and bruises. You lost your luster. You really stood out from the other apples. You were, in a sense, damaged goods. You felt worthless. You expected to be thrown out any day.

Then, one day, instead of being discarded, you were picked up by someone who saw what you could become. They diced and sliced you and turned you into the most beautiful, tasty apple crumble.

Yes, you have been damaged and bruised. Yes, you stood out from others around you and lost your shine, but you can turn yourself into something else. You may not look like the apple you once were, but you're still a delightful and tasty one, an apple that people can still enjoy.

One reason I use this analogy is that my partner is a great baker. There have been times when she has caught me about to throw out damaged fruit, only for her to say, "Hey, wait a minute. I can use that!"

Then she adds, "Damaged fruit is the sweetest. I'll make apple crumble tonight!"

She's right—the apple crumble, or the banana cake made from old, bruised bananas, is always delicious.

So, yes, you'll have changed. Still, you can reinvent yourself into something wonderful!

Chapter 9:

Hard Days Can Soften

Hyacinth: Peace, forgiveness

When you're caught up in grief, the days are hard, and the nights are worse. But as you begin to heal, the days and nights will soften. You'll find interest in the days and comfort in the nights. You'll begin to recognize the sun and stars again. The clouds won't all pour rain. Your path will not be all dark.

Of course, there will still be difficult days and nights. Sometimes you will find yourself feeling the sadness you had when your loved one first died. Sometimes your heart will still hurt. But overall, the hard days do soften. Your loved one will never leave your mind, but now the memories become bearable. They may even bring you comfort.

But there are days that are especially difficult, such as anniversaries like birthdays and holidays, that send you right back to that place of pain. There are ways to lessen that pain, to ease your broken heart, and to open yourself to the possibility of a life that's not as hard.

The Hard Days

Among the hardest days are anniversaries. The anniversary of your loved one's death can pierce your heart for many years to come. It's something that you likely will never forget. Birthdays, too, are difficult, especially significant ones like the 21st or the 50th. You remember how you used to celebrate each year, giving presents, partying with friends, sharing a special meal or a favorite cake. The death of a child will evoke sorrow every year afterward.

Happy holidays when families get together for elaborate meals and gift-giving, games and songs, and time spent together doing everyday things like watching sporting events are unbearable when you recall that someone is missing. You may find yourself isolating from your family and friends, not wanting to see them enjoying the occasion while you're still caught up in bittersweet memories.

If you've lost a child, their death can bring up especially painful times. Whenever you read your other children's favorite books, go hiking in the woods with them, go to their school plays, or watch them graduating, you will feel deeply that one more child should be there. You try to put a brave face on it, but you're suffering—and the remaining children are, too.

The same holds true if it's not a family member who died. Each time your team wins a softball or bowling game, the memory of your best friend will remind you that they are not there to share the victory. You read a book and think, *John would have loved that* or see a movie and say to yourself, *I wish I could tell Kim about that*. You may have known the person well enough to predict what joke they would have made when something funny happens.

Even the deaths of people who aren't related to you can cause fresh pain. If you've lost a loved one to suicide or an accident, hearing about a similar tragedy will be a searing reminder of the death. A news story about the event can cause intense pain. If you've lost a person close to you to cancer, you may find it too difficult to visit someone in the hospital who has the same illness.

These are the hard days. They don't go away completely. But the edges of the pain will soften like the edges of a stone statue that is subject to countless years of wind and rain.

Misplaced Emotions

Big events aren't necessary to bring back the pain of a death, either. Something that has no apparent connection to your loved one can suddenly zap you with a feeling of grief. If you see a couple on the street holding hands, for example, you can experience a moment of anguish because you can no longer enjoy that closeness. You could also feel a pang of anger, though, at the thought that such a wonderful feeling is now closed to you. You aren't really angry at the couple holding hands—you don't even know them. But you feel anger, nonetheless.

You project the pain you're feeling onto the other person. This is an example of irrational thinking. You don't know the other couple and have no reason to be angry with them, but that doesn't make the emotion any less real. The pain is exactly the same.

If you've lost a child, there are even more opportunities for your emotions to take over in this way. Just walking through town and past a school, you will often see children laughing and playing in the schoolyard. You can feel jealousy or envy that they are able to enjoy themselves when your child can't be there with them. When you see a child wearing a Mickey Mouse shirt, you may experience regret that you were never able to take your own child to Disney World. These projected emotions of anger, sorrow, jealousy, envy, or regret are real to you even if there's no factual basis for them. You are recalling things that happened in times past or imagining ones that might have been but never will be.

How do you banish these ghostly feelings and move back into the reality of life without your loved one? How can you make the hard days less traumatic and the edges of the pain soften? There are rituals that can make the transition easier. If you try one or more of these techniques, you can dull the edges of your grief and introduce some peace into your heart.

Rituals for Healing

Many religions have traditions that serve to remember the departed and memorialize them. They're an essential step in both remembering your loved one and moving on with peace in your life. Some occur shortly after the funeral while others continue for a longer time. There are wakes, which can be either festive or melancholy, often featuring songs and stories that remind the participants of the loved one. Or there may be a viewing or visitation before the actual funeral service.

In Japan, the wake occurs before the funeral. There is sitting shiva, a Jewish tradition that involves seven days of ritual mourning by the immediate family. Friends and relatives visit to say prayers, and mirrors in the house are covered. Islamic mourning involves a 40-day mourning period, and no flowers are received. The Catholic rites feature a Mass or religious service for the soul of the deceased, along with lighting candles representing prayers. Many Protestant denominations bring food to a gathering of friends and loved ones to spare them the chore of cooking during the post-funeral period and to share fellowship. Buddhist mourners may wear black or white but not colored clothing, and the family may hold a reception for mourners to pay their respects.

Many people, however, choose less traditional or formal ways of memorializing the departed. Instead of ceremonies, they choose more personal ways to commemorate the life and express sorrow at the death of a friend or loved one. The unique relationships they shared are celebrated or mourned in ways that bring healing and peace to those left behind. Here are some that have helped me process grief and move on to a place of caring and memory without the crushing pain. Now, I'd like to share them with you. Feel free to use them as is or to add your own meaningful touches to them.

Ritual 1—Affirmations

Affirmations are brief statements you tell yourself to reinforce your good qualities and build up your strengths. Affirmations are a practice of positive thinking and self-empowerment. They often take the form of sentences, such as "I am a good friend," "I am compassionate," or "I deserve peace." They should be about three to seven words in length.

Affirmations train the brain to think in ways that will aid your growth and stability. When you repeat these statements aloud or write them down, you are reaching your subconscious through your senses and teaching your brain to know and believe that you have the ability to be good and do better.

Repetition and consistency create and reinforce a positive mental attitude. Because of that, most people say their affirmations twice a day so that the messages enter the mind through their sense of hearing. Often, people write their affirmations on sticky notes and place them around their bathroom mirror so they're the first thing they see in the morning and the last thing they see at night. You can also say your affirmations silently to yourself if you are in a public place such as at your desk at work. Other people prefer to keep a journal to write their affirmations in, using the sense of touch to reinforce the messages. You can even set a note and a reminder on your phone so you will be nudged to repeat your affirmations several times a day.

How do affirmations work in the context of healing from grief? Someone with intrusive negative thoughts about the death of a loved one can replace a thought such as *I can't get through this* with the affirmation *I am strong*. The thought *All I feel is pain* can be countered with the affirmation *I am capable of love*. Try to think of a statement that is opposite to the negative feeling you have. Then repeat it until you firmly believe it.

I use this strategy during the day when I might be having a particularly difficult moment where I need an emotional correction or adjustment.

Every day, probably for the past seven years or so, I rarely miss sitting down and writing positive affirmations. It's a great way to create a positive mental attitude each morning. While you can create affirmations of self-love verbally or mentally, I think the written form is the most effective for me. I say each word with conviction as I write. I'm using several senses (vision, hearing, touch), which makes this very impactful.

Here are some suggestions: Avoid using the words should, could, or must. Write in the present tense: "I am" or "I can" rather than "I did," unless you are reinforcing positive behavior you've carried out: "I was brave when I met Jean today." Ensure the affirmation is positive—no negativity. You don't say, "I couldn't go to the class reunion." Instead, say, "Next year, I will."

The affirmations must be credible and achievable. Don't push yourself too hard, too fast. Instead of saying, "I am going to be more social," say, "I will go walk in the park today." Instead of saying, "I am able to go to Michael's party," say, "I will call Michael tomorrow."

Most important is your focus. Clear your mind and believe in what you write or say as if it is what you already are or are capable of. The goal is to train your subconscious mind to think in terms of what you already are. I write for just five minutes—the same thought repeatedly. The next morning, I may change what I wish to affirm that day. Here's an example: "I am confident. I am powerful. I am strong. I am getting better every day." I repeat these affirmations for approximately five minutes.

Ritual 2—Love Letter

Writing a letter to a loved one who is no longer with you is a well-known spiritual practice. However, it doesn't matter what your belief system or religion is—or even if you have one. This ritual can be very powerful for anyone. Written expression can create a feeling of real connection with your loved one who has passed. During the process, people often describe a release of negative energy. The ritual can also involve burning the letter, which turns fire into a powerful symbol. Smoke rising up to the sky is often associated with words or wishes flying upward into another realm.

When my wife died, I found it difficult to accept that I couldn't just talk with her anymore. There was so much I still wanted to say. About two years after her death, I tried the letter-to-your-loved-one technique.

I sat down one day when I knew I wasn't going to be interrupted and wrote my letter. I wrote her name at the top, and I just started. I wrote all my regrets, my failures, and my guilt. I wrote about the magical times in our life together—the first time we met, our wedding night when I had her in my arms, running across the courtyard of the motel in the pouring rain, laughing our heads off. (This is still my most treasured memory.)

I wrote it all. I poured out all my feelings on tear-soaked paper. When I had finished, I signed my letter. Then I read it out loud. It was an incredible feeling of intense emotion—beautiful emotion. I went out into the backyard and set up a small brick fire pit. I read the letter softly to my wife again. Then, I placed the letter in the pit, lit it, and watched the smoke rise. I was visualizing all my words returning to my wife. It was so powerful for me, emotional in so many ways. I still treasure that beautiful moment of my outpouring expression of love for her.

Be aware, though: This process can be very emotional. You are using many of your senses, coupled with the process of burning and the meaning behind it. The surreal dynamic it creates can be truly magical. You can have someone present with you for emotional support if you wish, but this is your moment. You decide how to carry out the ritual. You can view it as a message for your loved one and contentment and resolution for you.

Ritual 3—Candle Reflection

There's another common practice that people have used to remember and channel beautiful thoughts and memories. It's often used at anniversaries and birthdays.

For this ritual, you select a quiet time on or near the anniversary, whether that's the anniversary of the death, a wedding anniversary, a birthday, or another significant moment. Find a place in your home or out of doors where you won't be interrupted. Gather a small candle and any objects that remind you of your loved one. When you light the candle, concentrate on the flame and the mementos surrounding it. Let your mind drift to pleasant memories that you and your loved one shared. Picture them in your mind. Or simply rest in the memories with your head bowed and your eyes closed—whatever feels right to you.

When you're finished with your meditation, take a deep, cleansing breath, blow out the candle, and conclude the ritual.

You can adapt this ritual in ways that feel best to you. Instead of a candle, you could focus on a single flower in a vase or a picture of your loved one. You could have soothing music playing or conduct the ritual in silence. You could even select a piece of music that was significant to your loved one. Build the ceremony around your memories of the person and what feels important to you. There is no one right way to do it. The object is both remembrance and peace.

When my father passed, my siblings and I received a small urn with his ashes, with my mother's blessing. I talked about it with my partner. We decided that it would be nice to have the urn in a special, somewhat private, place. We agreed on the top shelf of a bookcase in the sitting room.

Next to the urn, I placed three framed photos of my dad that were special to me. I went out and purchased a nice candle. On special anniversaries I go into the living room and light it. I talk to my dad as if he is standing next to me. I say how much I love him, how special he was to me, and how much I miss him. While I am speaking, I place one hand on the urn, and with the other, I caress his face in the photo. Then I look at the candle for a while before I blow it out. It feels good for me!

You might try a similar ritual—it does create a closeness. I hope your hard days will soften for you as you create a way of remembering a special occasion.

Chapter 10:

Memories Can Be Your Freedom

Christmas rose: Tranquility, peace, serenity

The memories you have of your departed loved one are treasures you'll never forget. You've experienced how those memories have brought you grief and sorrow. Now, it's time to look at how those memories will transform into something positive.

Thoughts of your dear friend or family member have the power to crystallize emotions within you. When you learn how to make those memories change from ones that bring you pain to ones that bring you healing, you will experience joy and gratitude from the same sources that once brought distress into your life. Transforming your pain in this way is very powerful as a source of healing.

Think how much more joy you'll have in your life when you can think back on the memories of your loved one and feel not grief but loving kindness and serenity. Does that sound impossible? You have the power within you to accomplish it. The process requires that you reframe your thoughts from ones of sadness to ones of peace and joyful remembrance. When this happens, your spirit will be truly healed.

When Will the Pain Go Away?

You've known the heartache of grief now. At times, it's seemed like it would last forever. Every day, a dozen little things have reminded you of your loved one and brought back a stab of pain. Listening to a song they loved can trigger sadness. Hearing their voice on their answering machine can make you burst into tears. Seeing a happy couple walking along the beach can bring on deep loneliness. Looking at photos of the good times you shared with your loved one has brought you deep pain because those times are gone. When the memories flood back, the pain is renewed. The hard days can be crushing.

It's impossible to say exactly when the pain will leave you. Even after you're fully healed, you may still experience a twinge of sorrow when something unexpectedly reminds you of your loved one. Pain and grief are so very personal that the change from sorrow to joy will happen in different ways for different people. And, as you know, there's no timeline for grief that tells you when the pain ought to be gone by.

Certain factors can influence how long you will experience the sadness and pain, however. The circumstances of your loved one's death will be a factor in how long you grieve intently. For example, the death of a child brings the most searing kind of grief, to family members, of course, but also to anyone who knew the child. There's something about an innocent life being cut short that is simply difficult to handle.

On the other hand, the death of an older person who has been suffering a long illness can be a peaceful passing that ends pain for your loved one and makes your own pain more understandable. You can look back on their life and your treasured memories of them, usually with a quicker resolution to grief.

Accidental death or death by suicide is especially difficult to deal with. It seems that the tumultuous feelings they cause will never resolve into peace. Anger, blame, guilt, and anguish form a background for all your actions and thoughts. The time it takes for grief to heal in these circumstances is often longer and the feelings more intense than with other kinds of death.

Your cultural background will also influence how you experience grief. In Mexican and other Hispanic cultures, for example, the celebration of the Day of the Dead allows family members to memorialize their loved one every year so that they won't be forgotten. The family has a small altar in their home with a picture of the departed, candles, incense, favorite foods, and meaningful possessions.

The Jewish Kaddish prayer is recited at funerals and by mourners but is also prayed for 11 months after the death and every year on the anniversary of the death. Many Jewish people will also leave a pebble on the gravestone of a loved one (or even a stranger) to indicate that the person has visited the grave and had thoughts of remembrance. The New Orleans jazz funeral procession starts with slow, mournful tunes but later breaks into upbeat music and dancing, becoming a joyful and vibrant event. Military funerals are solemn occasions, with "Taps" played on a single bugle and the flag that covered the casket folded in a certain pattern and given to family members to keep.

Having structured rituals such as these and others gives the mourners a time and place to express their grief, remember their loved one, and transform their pain into memories and blessings.

Everyone is different. Some find solace in their religious traditions while others rely on a philosophical interpretation of death. Whether you believe in an afterlife—and what kind—can also influence your perception of and reaction to death. There are many different spiritual, religious, and scientific beliefs about death, from an afterlife of perpetual bliss or punishment to reincarnation to no form of survival after death, and more besides.

All of these elements combine to form your reactions to death and help you recover from grief. None of them can completely take away your pain, but they can help you cope with the death and shorten the time span until sorrow heals and peace descends.

Finally, your thoughts about your loved one and the memories you've built together influence how you react to their death. Your brain processes your reactions to stimuli such as the sight of a photograph of your loved one. The stimulus is a trigger, but it can be a trigger for grief or for healing. When the death first occurred, seeing a photo of the two of you together will have brought feelings of loneliness and longing. After time has passed, the same photo will bring memories of warm feelings and good times spent together.

This process in which your brain changes to have a new reaction to the stimulus is profound. As you look at the photo, your mental interpretation will have changed over time. Your thoughts about it are the key to the transition from grief to healing.

Cognitive Interpretation

Cognitive interpretation means thinking about how you think and feel. You examine what's going on with your thoughts and emotions to determine what causes them and what you can do about them. For example, you can look at the triggers that affect your emotions and behavior.

You already know that triggers or stimuli can affect how you feel. You've no doubt experienced this often since your loved one died. The thought of anything that reminds you of them brings on emotions such as sadness, numbness, or even anger, depending on how far along you are on your journey through grief to healing. You interpret a picture of your dear friend or family member as a reminder of their death. You interpret walking through a park you both enjoyed as a stab of pain.

Whether it's a family occasion, seeing an empty place at the dinner table, the hustle and bustle you experience on vacation, hearing a child's laughter, or the sight of a couple lovingly holding hands across the table in a restaurant—any of these stimuli can trigger your thoughts and feelings.

What these stimuli have in common is that they can create immense heartbreak or other painful emotions. You may think that this will never change. But by reframing your thoughts, you can channel these stimuli into peaceful, pleasant emotions. Psychologists or other mental health workers can help you do this through cognitive behavioral therapy (CBT).

Cognitive Behavioral Therapy

What is CBT, and how can it help you? Let's look first at how CBT developed into the most popular form of therapy there is.

Behaviorist John B. Watson prepared the way for CBT as early as 1913, basing his work on that of B.F. Skinner, who is famous for his operant conditioning experiments involving changing the behavior of dogs through stimuli. Later, in the 1950s, Albert Ellis developed rational emotive behavior therapy, which taught clients to recognize their irrational thoughts. They were encouraged to confront these thoughts and adjust them to more rational ones. Finally, in the 1960s, Dr. Aaron T. Beck developed CBT. He noticed that depressed patients had negative thoughts such as those about themselves, the world, or the future, which seemed to arise automatically. His CBT helped them develop resilience (Miller, 2019).

Now, CBT is perhaps the most-used form of therapy. It's been used for treating conditions as different as nightmares, bed-wetting, obsessive-compulsive disorder, anxiety, and phobias, as well as grief. There are many reasons for CBT's popularity. First, it is a form of talk therapy that doesn't usually require medication and can be effective in cases where medication hasn't helped. Then, too, it doesn't take long to have an effect—from 5 to 20 sessions.

Because the techniques are very practical, learning them can help a patient cope with future stresses as well as the ones they're experiencing when they start CBT therapy. This kind of therapy can be delivered online, in person, in groups, and through aids such as workbooks. Some people even find that they can learn the principles of CBT by themselves.

Of course, in order for CBT to be effective, the person must be fully committed to the process. People who have other mental health difficulties already, such as bipolar disorder or PTSD, may have more difficulty using CBT. And while the therapy can be delivered in a few sessions, putting it into practice in your life can take more time.

One of the techniques used in CBT is to understand the stimulus or trigger for the thoughts and feelings, the negative thoughts that arise when you encounter the trigger, and the consequences of the negative behaviors you exhibit after you experience the negative thoughts. In a case of grief, a stimulus might be a photo of you and your loved one enjoying yourselves at a party. The negative thought might be that you will never be that happy again since your loved one isn't there to share it with you. The behavior might be that you stop going to enjoyable social gatherings.

In the theory of CBT, it isn't the actual stimulus that causes pain but the negative thoughts that misinterpret the trigger and lead to the behavior. To use the example, seeing the photo is not the real problem. Instead, the feeling of loneliness and despair that accompanies the thought that you'll never be happy again is the misinterpretation that leads to the behavior of avoiding other people. Once you understand this process, you're better able to short-circuit the misinterpreted thoughts that lead to negative emotions and actions.

Another therapy related to CBT is dialectical behavior therapy (DBT). It shares many characteristics with CBT but is usually a longer-term therapy, lasting a year or more. With DBT, you accept your negative emotions and feel them fully, eventually letting go of them. Acceptance and commitment therapy (ACT) is another alternative. In ACT, you notice and accept your negative thought patterns and even embrace them.

CBT is preferable to these other types of therapy because it is problem-oriented and deals with solutions to current problems rather than those that grow out of long-ago incidents. Of course, even addressing current problems can be stressful at first, so it's necessary to commit to CBT and stick with it as the effects grow more and more helpful. In essence, the goal of CBT is to move beyond the need for a therapist at all. Once you get the hang of the practice, you'll be able to continue on your own.

Reframing Thoughts

CBT involves getting in touch with your negative feelings about the stimuli or triggers you encounter so that you can then reframe them. Reframing thoughts is also known as "rescripting" or "restructuring" them. You can't change or remove the triggers or stimuli in your life, but you most certainly can challenge and change how you think about them. This cognitive correction, or reframing of thoughts, can bring about more positive feelings that result in desired behaviors. This is an important life skill that will greatly benefit you in the future.

First, let's look at how you can get in touch with your negative thoughts. At first, all you may know is that you feel psychological pain—sadness, emptiness, numbness, guilt, blame, and all the other feelings that you may not even be able to identify.

Journaling is one technique that can help you surface your feelings and behaviors. You can make a three-column chart, for example, heading the columns "trigger," "thought," and "behavior." The more information you can add to the chart, the better you will understand what's happening with you. You might have a page that says "Trigger: seeing my loved one's favorite flowers;" "Thought: they'll never be here to enjoy this again;" "Behavior: giving up gardening." Gardening may have brought you joy in the past, but now it only causes you pain.

One very basic technique that you can use focuses on the thought column of the journal. "Thought-stopping" is just that. You listen to your inner voice and identify the negative thought, in this case that your loved one will never be able to enjoy the flowers again. When you notice yourself thinking this, tell yourself, "No!" You can even say it aloud to reinforce the idea.

Many people confuse their inner voice with their conscience, but it's really not the same. Inner voice, also known as "self-talk," is the series of running thoughts that you think all day long. Most of them are ordinary, like *I need to pick up cheese at the store*. But in the case of grief, your inner voice will be telling you the negative thoughts about your emotions.

After thought-stopping comes reframing. This step will take commitment and practice because you are trying to retrain the brain. It's not a procedure most people are familiar with. In your journal chart, the first column—the trigger—remains the same. The second column is where you do the work. You transform the negative thought into a positive one. You still have the same sensation that triggered you, but you replace your automatic reaction to it with something else, something more in line with healing.

Let's take a look at the triggers, negative emotions, and behaviors that we discussed earlier.

The first example was of a person looking at a photo of their loved one and thinking, *I miss them terribly. I wish I could hold them.* The trigger and the negative thought or emotion are easy to identify. How could you reframe the negative emotion? Instead of thinking about what will never happen again, you could find yourself thinking, *I treasured every moment with them and loved holding them. I feel so blessed.* This new way of speaking about the trigger and the emotion is a result of a change in your brain. You are now free to remember the good times without dwelling on how much you've lost.

Another trigger may have been attending a family event and thinking simply, *I wish they were here.* Your reframed thought might be a pleasant memory: *I remember how they used to make faces at the table when they were bored. That really cracked me up!* Instead of staying away from holiday gatherings, you can now go and share your memories with your other loved ones.

When you notice an empty chair at the dinner table, you may have the negative reaction of *I am so lonely without you.* Reframed in light of your healing from grief, you might think instead, *We had an amazing life together. I wouldn't change a thing.*

Perhaps you used to go on vacation with your loved one and think you can never go on a vacation again without them because it just wouldn't be the same. After reframing your thoughts, you might remember, *When we were on vacation, you were sleeping in the back seat of the car as we traveled and your farts used to wake you up. You tried to claim it was me. Then you would go back to sleep, and I would chuckle for the next hour.* Remembering the silliness and the laughter will be powerful antidotes to the depths of the blues. The next time you go on away on holiday, you may find yourself giggling at the memory.

It may have been especially hard on you to hear a child's laughter. It was easy to think, *My daughter would have been just that age* and to avoid places where happy children might be playing. Your sad emotions will start to build up, even to the point that it causes you to cry. Reframing your thought means that your reaction will be, *My darling child, because of you, I will make my life count!* Your sorrow will be transformed into a resolution to improve your life and do something worthwhile with it— a beautiful memorial to your departed child.

When you see a couple holding hands, you may have thought, *I hate seeing this! I wish that was us again.* After working through your grief with CBT, you may find yourself saying instead, *That makes me smile. I always had a special feeling when we held hands in public.*

It may take practice for you to learn how to reframe your thoughts. That journal you're keeping with the columns for trigger, thought, and behavior can have two new columns: reframed thought and changed behavior. Go back through the situations and thoughts you've noticed and think about how you could reframe them into something positive. Don't think of it as forgetting or letting go of your loved one. It really helps to honor them in a very special way that makes you feel closer instead of dwelling on the loss.

Making CBT Work for You

While you can find online guides and workbooks for CBT, it is so much better to do the therapy under the care of a qualified mental health worker. The principles behind the theory may seem simple at first, but they can prove difficult to learn, practice, and maintain. Someone with training in how to implement CBT is a valuable resource as well as a helper. They can guide you along the way and help when you experience difficulties in the process. They can help you keep going if you get stuck along the way. And they can provide a safe space for you to explore your feelings. Most of all, they are there to listen to you and guide you through the CBT experience. Everyone's experience of grief is different, and a mental health professional will understand your particular situation.

It's important that you reach a certain stage of grief before CBT will be effective. The first, most painful and devastating feelings must pass for you to be ready to recognize your negative thoughts and behaviors and to reframe them. You need to have a level of emotional awareness and healing to make CBT work for you. The principles involved won't make sense until you are ready to take them in and put them into practice.

You also have to commit to the work of CBT. And it is work! It takes sustained effort to learn how to be aware of what your inner voice is saying to you, understand how those thoughts hold you back, and see your way clear to changing your way of thinking. It can be frustrating and even tiring, even if you use a visual aid such as your chart of triggers, thoughts, behaviors, and reframed thoughts. The transformation won't happen overnight. While it could take as few as five weekly sessions to get the hang of it, it may require more, depending on your personal situation. You have to be willing to invest the time and effort in order to make progress.

Finally, it's important to be open to the joyous, peaceful, or even funny moments that will occur to you. Your thoughts will not all be solemn. They'll be personal to you and your loved one and can be quite endearing. They may be unexpectedly amusing. Some of them will be lighthearted and even ridiculous. But those thoughts are what it takes to break through the walls of sorrow that have been holding you back. Embrace those happy thoughts. Above all, CBT should make you feel grateful and blessed for the presence of this person in your life. After all, you've decided that your loved one's legacy will not be one of perpetual sorrow!

CBT takes some time and some hard work. After all, you're reprogramming the most complex part of your body—your brain. The billions of connections within this sophisticated computer are what carry your memories. Retraining them will not happen rapidly. Be gentle with yourself and take whatever time you need for your brain to learn new ways of thinking and better ways of expressing the love you still feel for your beloved friend or family member.

Sadness Becomes Joy

It will be a truly amazing experience when the brain and thoughts that once brought you so much sorrow, grief, and pain are retrained and reframed. Your sensibilities will be renewed, and you'll see the world through a new lens of happiness. Now, you'll have a real, lasting sense of appreciation, joy, and gratitude for living life with your loved one. Your memories will bring you comfort instead of distress.

Of course, sadness may linger. That's only natural. But it won't take over your life forever, as you may have thought it would. If you continue to challenge and reframe your painful thoughts, sorrow will dissipate, leaving room for joy to grow and flourish. The emotions that will now fill your days and nights will be joy, appreciation, and gratitude. The grief you've experienced is dark, but it can lighten. And memories will build your freedom from grief!

Conclusion

Cosmos: From the Greek word Kosmos, *which translates as "being in harmony";*
balanced and in harmony

I hope this book has helped you with the grief that dealing with the death of a loved one can bring. I've tried to make it as understandable and practical as possible. In my practice as a mental health worker, I've encountered many people who are suffering the effects of grief. It has disrupted their lives and caused them untold sorrow and pain. I want to help lessen that sorrow and help people get back to the lives they lived before death intruded.

Of course, it's impossible to fully eliminate the feelings that accompany grief. You never forget your dear friend or beloved family member—nor should you. You'll always remember their death. But you can also remember your love for them and the good times you had together without the pain of grief taking over and making you suffer excessively.

There are certain aspects of grief I've tried to stress. Here's a look at the path I've outlined. The first principle is that there is no timetable for grief. Everyone experiences it in their own way. Working through the feelings will take as long as it takes for every person. Don't let anyone tell you that you're grieving wrong or for too long or inappropriately. You feel your grief as an individual, even if there are people around you who share it. Each of them is grieving in their own way and in their own time, too.

Your grief doesn't have to consume your life. You can heal. You can embrace the rest of your life without the sorrow and misery you have felt. Through a process of healing, you'll be able to leave the negative feelings behind while still holding on to the positive ones.

When you first learn of the death, you'll naturally go into a state of psychological shock. This is normal. There is a series of feelings that you'll go through. It may not be the traditional five stages of grief you've no doubt heard about, and you don't have to go through the stages in the same order as someone else. But at some point, you'll experience disbelief and denial. Later come confusion, anger, bargaining, projection, panic, and guilt.

Feeling these emotions hurts you terribly, but they are necessary steps toward healing. After all, you can only start to heal after you feel. Repressing or denying your emotions only postpones the start of healing and prolongs your feelings of pain. A person who can support you emotionally while you're processing your feelings is a treasure. Many people will instead tell you how you ought to feel. Ignore them if you can and continue along your personal process of healing.

You've no doubt experienced the exhausting rituals of the funeral, especially if you were the one responsible for making all the arrangements. There were responsibilities to shoulder before, during, and after the funeral, and that hasn't been easy. In fact, it has been exhausting and draining. Even positive memories may cause you pain because you experienced those events in the past and realize they will never come again.

The stress caused by the funeral affects you deeply. After all, the details you have to deal with are exhausting. It's only natural that you were exhausted both physically and emotionally. You may have negative feelings about the way other friends and relatives have reacted to the death. But remember that each of them is grieving in their own way, just as you have been.

There are resources available to you to make the many tasks easier for you. Your family doctor and the funeral director are important, so are supportive friends and relatives. Also, remember that there are many support groups available for grieving people, and you can get in touch with them at any stage of the process, not only when your grief is recent and fresh.

Loneliness is likely one of the many emotions you've experienced since the death of your loved one, whether you live with others or are living alone. Even with a large circle of friends who also knew your beloved friend or family member, you can still feel alone.

Developing a routine or distracting your mind with other activities may help you when the loneliness becomes too great, but you may also consult a mental health professional. They know how to treat grief disorders and help people who've experienced a loss process their emotions and begin to find their way back to life. They use active listening to help identify what you are feeling and develop the best strategies for your particular situation.

However, you may experience setbacks along the way. You might feel ready to resume social engagements but find they are still too painful. Easing into them gradually will likely be more effective. Finding ways to tell friends and relatives that you are still having difficulties may be particularly difficult.

While everyone's timeline for grief is different, when you make no progress in dealing with your emotions, you may develop anxiety or depression, which can be very serious. A mental health professional can help, and medication could even be prescribed.

At last, you may have begun to experience glimmers, flashes of momentary joy or appreciation of nature that you have noticed. These are a sign of beginning to heal and have been good for your spirit. Paradoxically, glimmers may have also caused you setbacks because you feel guilty about feeling a sense of lightness, even if it's just a flash. But you are the one ready to experience the glimmers, to know when and where to look for them. You are the one creating your new reality after your experience of grief.

If those glimmers lead to good memories of your loved one, so much the better! Sense memories, those that incorporate touch, taste, sound, and scents as well as sight, are even more powerful. On the other hand, these powerful memories can lead you back to the beginning of your processing of grief. These feelings will come and go, compared with the consistent intense pain and sorrow you felt when your loved one's death was fresh.

You may feel stuck because of the setbacks, but in reality, you are now poised for an awakening. Your brain has experienced a change. Frustration with your seeming lack of progress has you primed to move on to another level of healing. You can't force or hurry this moment; it will happen when you're emotionally ready for it. Your mind switches on and you realize that your loved one would not want their legacy to be one of misery. You are experiencing one of the most amazing phases of healing—the ability to move to a different level, one in which your mind is once again open to joy.

With that awakening, you'll begin to gain more confidence and to re-engage with the world around you. Although it may seem difficult at first, you'll be able to try doing the things you used to love. It's not a betrayal of your loved one. It's a renewal of life within you and an opportunity to explore activities that energize your body and brain. As you do gain confidence, you'll discover which ones you want to be part of the new life that is opening up. There will be changes, but you'll be ready to embrace them.

There will still be difficult days, of course. The anniversary of your loved one's death will bring up powerful memories, a mixture of both nostalgia and pain. Just as you have experienced glimmers of light, you will also encounter moments of darkness, times when sights and sounds around you remind you of the past. Irrational thoughts arise, making your negative emotions return temporarily. You can create your own rituals for healing, however—ones that allow you to let go of the pain you've felt and keep the good memories you have stored up.

If you're still having trouble with negative emotions and intrusive thoughts, you may find help through cognitive behavioral therapy. It can help you examine your thoughts and feelings, realize which ones are not helping you to heal, and reframe the ones that are causing you the most setbacks. When you reframe your thoughts, you gain a fresh perspective on the things that have been causing you pain and learn how to shift your view to something healthier and more positive.

Your feelings are a work in progress, and you've come a long way from the early days when the death of your beloved friend or family member left you trapped in pain and misery. You are now learning to live again in happiness and joy.

Death isn't the only cause of grief, however. In the second book in this series, I'll look at grief associated with major life issues, including depression, anxiety disorder, divorce and separation, estrangement, and poverty and financial hardship. The grief associated with these major life issues differs from grief associated with the death of a loved one. I'll look deeper into an individual's cognitive comprehension, developing an understanding of how our minds work. Through self-discovery and a comprehensive emotional awareness, we are able to address the grief associated with distressing life issues. These can leave you feeling confused and cause suffering, too. Finding your way back from the pain you feel can take time and effort.

Another form of grief you may encounter is called "prolonged grief disorder," when complicated grief lasts so long that it impairs your ability to continue with your daily life. In the final book of the series, I'll look at prolonged grief and grief associated with tragic life events including death at the hands of another, suicide, loss in early life, and chronic incapacitation. The grief associated with traumatic death or tragic life events is quite complex. There are heightened emotions that do require a great deal of time and usually professional intervention to resolve. With the second and third books in this series, I'll delve deeper into cognitive comprehension and offer guidance with the strategies required to regain purpose in life.

I hope that, if you're suffering from any of those manifestations of grief, you'll turn to me. I can help. You can return to life and joy, and I'm ready to show you the way!

Book Review

Dear Reader, it has been my privilege to walk with you and guide you at this difficult time.

I trust I was able to show how there can be peace in your life again.

If you found solace in my book, I will be forever grateful if you could leave me a Review.

A moment of your time can encourage more people to benefit from this content.

The QR codes below will direct you to the Review Page or Home Page of this book in your country/marketplace. You can find "Customer Reviews" or "Review this product" on the left-hand side of the Book's Homepage. Your feedback is greatly appreciated.

Thank you.

USA

UK

Canada

Australia

References

Boyes, A. (2018, March 6). *What is psychological shock? And 5 tips for coping.* Psychology   Today. https://www.psychologytoday.com/us/blog/in-practice/201803/what-is-psychological-shock-and-5-tips-coping

Cuncic, A. (2022, November 9). *What is active listening?* Verywell Mind. https://www.verywellmind.com/what-is-active-listening-3024343

The   five   stages   of   grief. (2022,   June   7).   Psycom. https://www.psycom.net/stages-of-grief

Funeral   customs   by   religion,   ethnicity   and   culture. (n.d.).   Funeralwise. https://www.funeralwise.com/funeral-customs/funeral-traditions-and-practices/

Goldman, R. (2022, November 4). *Affirmations: What they are and how to   use   them.*   Everyday   Health. https://www.everydayhealth.com/emotional-health/what-are-affirmations/

Grief and the role of the funeral director. (n.d.). National Mortuary Shipping   &   Cremation. https://www.natlmortuaryshipping.com/news/grief-and-the-role-of-the-funeral-director

Grief care: How funeral homes provide additional support after the service. (2020, October 26). Vertin. https://www.vertin.com/grief-care-how-funeral-homes-provide-additional-support-after-the-service/

Herrity, J. (2018). *Active listening skills: Definition and examples.* Indeed. https://www.indeed.com/career-advice/career-development/active-listening-skills

Holland, K. (2018, September 25). *Stages of grief: General patterns for breakups, divorce, loss, more.* Healthline Media. https://www.healthline.com/health/stages-of-grief

Jo, A. (2022, April 6). *Funeral service and grief work: How to support grieving families.* Connecting Directors. https://connectingdirectors.com/63071-funeral-service-and-grief-work

Khan, A. (2018, July 27). *What you should know about shock.* Healthline Media. https://www.healthline.com/health/shock

Mayo Clinic Staff. (2022, December 13). *Complicated grief—Symptoms and causes.* Mayo Clinic. https://www.mayoclinic.org/diseases-conditions/complicated-grief/symptoms-causes/syc-20360374

Miller, K. (2019, June 19). *CBT explained: An overview and summary of CBT.* Positive Psychology. https://positivepsychology.com/cbt/

Milne, B. (2022, September 1). *Complete checklist for what to do after someone dies.* Better Place Forests. https://www.betterplaceforests.com/blog/end-of-life-planning/complete-checklist-for-what-to-do-after-someone-dies/

Wisner, W. (2018, November 7). *How dangerous is denial?* Talkspace. https://www.talkspace.com/blog/how-dangerous-is-denial/

Image References

Betexion. (2021, February 20). *White poppy* [Image]. Pexels. https://www.pexels.com/photo/close-up-shot-of-a-white-poppy-in-bloom-6899026/

Boks, K. (2021, July 9). *A lotus flower in bloom* [Image]. Pexels. https://www.pexels.com/photo/a-lotus-flower-in-bloom-8685419/

Grabowska, K. (2020, April 21). *Close up photo of purple flowers* [Image.] Pexels. https://www.pexels.com/photo/close-up-photo-of-purple-flowers-4207490/

Hamm, M. (2020, July 23). *Lavender* [Image]. Unsplash. https://unsplash.com/photos/purple-flower-in-macro-shot-je_1U2YSIho

Hans. (2015, November 18). *Christmas rose* [Image]. Pixabay. https://pixabay.com/photos/christmas-rose-anemone-blanda-flower-1024872/

Marisa04. (2018, May 23). *Peony* [Image]. Pixabay. https://pixabay.com/photos/peony-flower-plant-common-peony-3424255/

MabelAmber. (2018, September 23). *Cosmos flower* [Image]. Pixabay. https://pixabay.com/photos/cosmea-flwoer-cosmos-pink-flower-3694471/

Olga_968. (2015, March 23). *Chamomile flowers* [Image]. Pixabay. https://pixabay.com/photos/chamomile-flowers-bloom-685582/

Peggychoucair. (2019, March 17). *White rose* [Image]. Pixabay. https://pixabay.com/photos/roses-blossoms-rose-blossom-white-4059127/

PublicDomainPictures. (2012, March 3). *Hyacinth* [Image]. Pixabay. https://pixabay.com/photos/field-flowers-grape-hyacinth-21687/

Santana, T. (2020, May 11). *Peace lily* [Image]. Pexels. https://www.pexels.com/photo/tender-peace-lily-flower-with-white-petal-4378078/

TanteTati. (2016, May 12). *Pincushion flower* [Image] Pixabay. https://pixabay.com/photos/glossy-scabiosis-shiny-scabiosis-1383822/